CW00468668

MEDSTEAD AND
FOUR MARKS

The Mid-Hants Railway

From Construction to Closure

By
Roger Hardingham

Roger Hardingham

Published by
Runpast Publishing
10 Kingscote Grove, Cheltenham, Gloucestershire GL51 6JX

For
Grace Lois Hardingham

The era that brings back many memories for people was the period when 'M7' Class tank locomotives pushed and pulled their two coaches along the line. Here, No. 30125 is at Alresford in 1958. *Mike Esau*

Designed by Roger Hardingham

ISBN 1 870754 29 8 1995
Printed By The Amadeus Press, Huddersfield, West Yorkshire

Contents

Acknowledgements

Any book of this nature cannot be compiled without the help and assistance of others. I have been particularly fortunate in receiving information and photographic illustrations from a good many people, many of whom have a keen interest in the Mid-Hants Railway. I would like to thank Chris Small of Alton for his huge list of observations by the lineside from the 1950s until closure of the railway, as these gave a remarkable record of traffic movements. Occasionally he also came up with 'a little gem' of a photograph taken by either his father, Rob Small, or himself.

A big thank you to Charles Lewis, a director of the preservation company in the early years. Without his initial collecting of archives of the railway and his vast collection of newspaper cuttings, the account of the run-up to closure would have been difficult. I am most grateful to those who came up with some excellent photographs, many at short notice, of a railway not known for its photographic coverage. The Winchester Museums Service thankfully had a rare collection of construction photographs in their archives and I would like to thank them for making these available. A colleague, Ron Neal, provided some fascinating views of the railway around the closure period and fortunately took some views of hitherto unseen areas of the line. Others I would like to thank for their assistance are; Philip Buckell; Mrs A.E. Colliver, whose father worked at Alresford and Ropley prior to 1931; Mrs M. Blythe, now in her 90s and who remembers events at Alresford before the First World War; Chris Cornell; John Elliott; David Foster-Smith for the rare photographs of the construction of the Meon Valley Railway; Bill Hurst; Jim Pitt; The Public Records Office; Tony Cross of the Curtis Museum, Alton; British Rail; Hampshire Records Office. I am most indebted to Peter Bancroft who has written the first chapter concerning the construction period. He has painstakingly researched these early times for his articles in the preservation society's magazine and I am most grateful to him for adapting them to this book. A great friend of the railway, the late Peter Cooper, studied locomotive history in some detail and his notes of the 'M7s' at work on the line were found in time by his wife Sue to include in the book.

Introduction

The documentation of any railway subject is of immense importance to present and future generations. When the subject is of such a close nature to so many people, it becomes even more important for the history to be written down and if possible, made accessible.

The Mid-Hants Railway is fortunate in having survived, in part, from the British Railways Beeching era of line closures and due to its survival, there are many people, enthusiasts and general public alike, who take a great interest in its past history and its future as an amenity in Hampshire. Today the line serves as a reminder of its past role in the railway infrastructure of the area, and can be enjoyed by many thousands of local people and visitors to Hampshire.

It is with its past history that this book will investigate, the story of preservation being left to another future publication. The line was in regular use for over 107 years, serving the local population between Alton and Winchester and travellers from London and the South West when it acted as a main line alternative to the nearby London to Southampton railway.

A neat gas lamp-post, doubling up as a signpost at Alresford in 1972. The 'totem' signs are now very sought after. *R. Neal*

When plans were being drawn up for the 'new' London and Southampton Railway Company's (the forerunner of the London & South Western Railway) line from London to the port, Francis Giles, the engineer for the LSR, was asked to survey a route. He produced two alternative lines of railway in his report of December 1830, one of which would take the tracks through Guildford, Farnham, Alton, Alresford and Winchester. His plan included a tunnel "between Alton and Alresford, of nearly three miles in length".

Both schemes were costed out at about £1,200,000 each, but as we now know, the line eventually went through Basingstoke. How different the economy would be now in the areas of Alton and Alresford if his first plan had been adopted. Another proposal, in 1845, this time by Joseph Locke the new engineer appointed by the LSR, was for a line to continue from the then proposed Guildford to Alton line. This would again continue via Alresford to Winchester to join the then built main line to Southampton. A tunnel was also envisaged through the hills to the west of Alton.

The seeds were beginning to be sown in the late 1850s for the Mid-Hants line as we know it ; a reference in the Court of Directors minutes of the LSWR for 8th June 1860 mentions a letter from Messrs Dunn, Hopkin & Co (solicitors) dated 28th May, "as to a line of railway from Alton through Titchborne to Winchester". The Directors elected not to back the plan and "declined to be entertained for the present" was the reply sent back. Chapter one will take up the story of progress in late 1860. Some twenty years before the Alton to Winchester line was opened, Britain was in the midst of the 'railway mania' period. In the mid 1840s hundreds of new schemes were put to Parliament for approval involving thousands of miles of track. During the two years from 1845 for example, twenty-five schemes were created involving the then town of Southampton alone. Although most did not of course achieve their aims it does illustrate the speculative period and the aspirations of companies and promoters of the time.

So, when the Alton, Alresford and Winchester Railway Company launched its plan for a line across mid Hampshire in 1861, many at the time must have wondered what the promoter's reasons were for such a railway, to be constructed well after the 'mania' period. The reasons were usually financial of course and as we shall see in the first two chapters, finances would play a pivotal role in the railway's first years.

There is no doubt that confidence in new schemes was lacking in the the 1860s and investors were few and far between. The projected line from Petersfield to Bishops Waltham to connect with Southampton via the Botley line fell by the wayside due to a total lack of investors, who had lost all hope of earning dividends from new projects.

The Alton, Alresford and Winchester Railway (as it was known in the early period) did, however, find the money to build its line and by 2nd October 1865 construction had advanced sufficiently to open the line to traffic. It served the people of Alton, Medstead, Ropley, Alresford, Itchen Abbas and surrounding areas until 1973 when, under British Railways, it had to close, albeit after one of the most intensive and protracted appeals in recent railway history.

Change of identity

On 29th July 1864, whilst construction of the Alton to Winchester line was proceeding apace, an Act was passed allowing the A,A&WR Co to change its name (from January 1865) to The Mid-Hants Railway Company. The Act also incorporated a new scheme to build a line from a junction with the current project at Ropley southwards to join up with the proposed extension from Petersfield to Bishop's Waltham (contained in a separate Act also dated 29th July 1864). The MHR was clearly setting its sights high in anticipation of the opening of the Alton to Winchester railway.

However, even after a revised scheme surveyed by Mr Tolme (the MHR engineer) to take the line south from a point at Alresford (near Jacklyn's Lane) towards Cheriton and then to Exton, the new line, known as 'the Mid-Hants Line' (the line being constructed was known as 'the Alton Line') was abandoned by an Act in 1869. This followed a meeting of the MHR Board on 27th May 1869 chaired by John Taylor (see how this name comes up again 100 years later in Chapter Seven) and after having votes cast by the current shareholders, most of whom assented to the abandonment. Shares held were listed as; Benjamin Bateman, £5,000; Edward Knight, £16,650; J.H. Tolme, £1,000 with twenty-eight others with lesser amounts. The Petersfield line's 12-mile extension had been abandoned in 1868.

Whenever motive power is considered on the Mid-Hants Railway, the 'M7' Class locomotives are usually recalled. These Victorian engines were built by the London & South Western Railway for branch line work and they played a crucial role on the line from 1937 to 1957. Prior to this and at times throughout the railway's life, practically every type of locomotive in service at the time must have worked over the line. As we shall see the early examples of Dugald Drummond, the LSWR's Locomotive Superintendent from 1895 to 1912, all traversed the line; the popular 'T9s' to name just one example were regulars. It is hard to imagine now what the scene at the time of opening in 1865 must have looked like, with local people in period costume and a rake of carriages with a locomotive at the head from one of the classes developed by Joseph Beattie.

The operation of services was the responsibility of the LSWR from the beginning; full responsibility being taken on when they bought the line outright in 1884. Quite early on the railway was given the nickname of 'the Alps' due to the relatively steep inclines, particularly in the area of Medstead & Four Marks and this was always a consideration when rostering locomotives. This factor would also attract its fair share of mishaps over the years, so many in fact, that a chapter is devoted to accidents on the line.

'700'Class No. 30350 arrives at Medstead & Four Marks station in the 1950s with a freight from Alton - the goods train was a feature of the line for most of its life. *R. Neal collection*

Chapter One

The Birth of a New Railway in Hampshire

This chapter has been written and researched by Peter Bancroft, who is painstakingly investigating the early years of the railway. His quest for more information on this period continues for future reference.

The early history of any railway company, large or small, is punctuated by several significant events, most of which are documented in one form or another. Often a prospectus was issued at an early date and this probably followed a local meeting of parties interested in, or likely to gain from, construction of a railway between two points. Eventually an Act of Parliament would be gained and deposited plans and sections would have accompanied this. A 'Book of Reference' citing the owners, occupiers and lessees of land on which the railway was to be built, would also be part of the submission to Parliament.

An Act of Parliament was needed in the first place, because the railway company were in effect asking for powers which were in excess, or in conflict with, the general law. Accompanying the Act might have been a subscription contract, giving details of a number of individuals who were willing to subscribe capital to construct the railway. These individuals are truly the promoters of the railway. Some might have gone on to become directors or officers of the company or some might have been landowners.

What usually tends to fill in many of the information gaps between these specific events, and to record progress on several other important areas, are the Board Minutes of the railway company. These would record the dates of meetings and detail any resolutions passed, contracts signed or sealed, resignations and appointments of Directors. The disappointment therefore, in the case of the Mid-Hants Railway Company (which of course started out as the Alton, Alresford and Winchester Railway Company) is that these minutes do not appear to have survived. There are as a result many blank pages in what might otherwise be an interesting and informative history, tracing the true origins of the Mid-Hants Railway. The most detailed account to be found of the independent days of the Mid-Hants, up till it was finally taken over by the LSWR on 30th June 1884, is that contained in *The London & South Western Railway Volume Two,* by R.A. Williams (David & Charles, 1973). It is clear though that much of this is researched from the LSWR's minutes (which have survived) and obviously records the story from their perspective. Thus the account cannot show in detail the Mid-Hants side of the story, because it does not exist in minute book form.

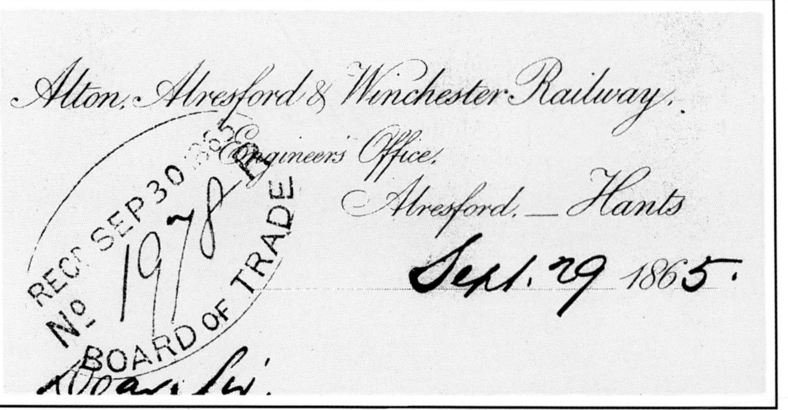
Alton, Alresford & Winchester Railway.
Engineers' Office,
Alresford, Hants
Sept. 29 1865.
RECD SEP 30 1865 No 1978 BOARD OF TRADE

A letterheading from the A,A&WR Co. of September 1865. This had an Alresford address, but others had 4 Victoria Street, Westminster, London.

Much of the early history of the Mid-Hants must therefore be gleaned from other sources of information. Bradshaw's Shareholders' Manuals, local newspapers and other railway journals. There are also a significant number of original documents at the Hampshire Record Office which shed light on the subject.

Williams, in his book, mentions that the London & South Western Railway had, on 20th September 1845, instructed its engineer, Joseph Locke, to survey a line in the area between Alton and Winchester. But if nothing seems to have come from this instruction, the idea was certainly not forgotten. In the meantime, the LSWR had reached Alton itself on 28th July 1852 with a single track from Farnham.

Of the A,A&WR Co. records which survive, the earliest item is a letter dated 4th October 1860 which was sent to John Wood Esq., of Thedden Grange, from Messrs Pain & Rawlins (solicitors) asking for his support for a railway from Alton through Alresford to a point near Winchester. Plans and sections had already been prepared by that time. Wood was one of the principal landowners affected by the line and his name was eventually added to the list of promoters. On 10th November 1860, the *Hampshire Chronicle, Southampton and Isle of Wight Courier,* published the first notice stating powers to build a railway would be sought in the next Parliamentary session. The Plans and Book of Reference were deposited at the Private Bill Office of the House of Lords on 30th November 1860. On 20th December 1860, J.E. Errington signed the Estimate of Expense for the line in the sum of £150,000. The following day this estimate was deposited at the same office, along with a List of Lessees, Occupiers and Owners of the land on which the railway was to be built. The A,A&WR Act of 1861 received its Examiners Certificate for compliance with Standing Orders in the House of Lords on 14th February 1861.

A preliminary meeting of the Directors of the company was called for one o'clock precisely on Wednesday 27th February 1861, to be held at the Swan Hotel, Alresford. Mr W. Rawlins (a solicitor) was acting as Secretary 'protem'. It was probably at that meeting that the wording of the prospectus was agreed and this appeared soon afterwards. Once again the *Hampshire Chronicle* was used as a means of advertising the project, with the first advert appearing on 2nd March 1861. The Prospectus contained, among others, the following names of Promoters: Rt Hon Lord Sherborne; Rt Hon Lord Ashburton; Sir James Francis Doughty Titchborne, Bart; Sir James Buller East, Bart, MP; Guildford Onslow Esq, MP; John Bonham Carter Esq, MP; The Mayor of Winchester. The promoters also included local businessmen and names which would become associated with the running of the Company: Edward Knight, Chairman; Robert Cole, Deputy Chairman; Jacob Hagen; Henry Hall; The Rev. J.T. Maine; Henry Joyce Mulock and John Wood.

The A,A&WR Act was passed on 28th June 1861. With this came the appointment of six Directors (the last named people, apart from The Rev J.T. Maine). The Act allowed for the construction of a railway from Alton to Winchester, including powers to raise capital and stipulated rates for the carriage of passengers, animals and goods. Powers were also granted for the Company to enter into a traffic agreement with the LSWR and for the LSWR to subscribe, if they wished, for up to £25,000 in shares in the Company. These last points were a sure indication that both companies realised that they would have to work closely together, because of the interworking and the need for a junction with the LSWR main line near Winchester. There appears also to have been a clear understanding from the start that the A,A&WR Co was to build the line only, with the LSWR providing the rolling stock and staff.

Just over a week later, at a Board meeting held on 6th July 1861, the Directors expressed concern at the 1 in 60 gradients and deep cuttings through Windmill Hill. Mr J.E. Errington, the Company's first engineer, was asked to survey an alternative route. The result presented to the Board in October 1861 was for a line of 1 in 75 gradient and a 880 yard long tunnel and on a different alignment through Chawton Park. The proposed deviation would have left the existing route at the Butts and taken a more northerly course to go through Chawton Park and round the north side of Windmill Hill. However, this would have necessitated a further application to Parliament and resulted in an additional cost of about £25,000. It was not ultimately recommended by Errington, who felt that the 1 in 60 gradients were not unreasonable in the circumstances. (The proposed tunnel should not be confused with the one in the same vicinity which had been proposed by the London & Southampton Railway, who had surveyed a line in the same area in the 1830s.)

John Edward Errington was born in Hull on 29th December 1806 and became an associate of the engineer Joseph Locke. He was involved in many railway projects in England and Scotland before

One of a rare collection of Mid-Hants Railway construction photographs which survive in the Savage collection at Winchester City Museum. Although Lovedon Lane bridge in the distance has been constructed to allow double track, the very steep chalk cuttings have only been dug to accommodate a single line. Soon trains would travel this stretch of line. *Winchester Museums Service*

Above: A view from the top of the embankment by the 3-arched Lovedon Lane bridge (sometimes referred to Stoke Charity) circa 1865. This is a photograph looking due east on the very straight section of line between Itchen Abbas and Winchester Junction. The Basingstoke main road bridge is in the far distance. *Below:* The bridge crossing the main Winchester road at the western end of Alresford. Note the culvert on the right carrying the Titch river. *Both, Winchester Museums Service*

moving to London at about the time Locke fell out with the Directors of the LSWR. Errington then stepped into the shoes of Locke as engineer to the 'South Western and went on to superintend the extension of the line from Yeovil to Exeter.

His involvement with the Mid-Hants scheme was quite short-lived and his main responsibility was to estimate the costs of construction and complete the original survey of the course. He died on 4th July 1862 after a short illness, leaving his task to two of his 'pupils', Messrs Galbraith and Tolme. They were appointed by the larger 'South Western Company, but the A,A&WR Co decided to offer Tolme, alone, the post. Julian Horne Tolme was born in Havana, Cuba on 28th January 1836. He came to England, with his father who was a merchant, in 1851. He became a student at King's College, London, studying geology and mineralogy and attended civil engineering classes. In 1855 he was articled for five years to Messrs Locke and Errington, with particular direction under Errington, then Engineer-in-Chief to the LSWR. Upon Errington's death Tolme (then just 26 years old) and Galbraith entered into partnership for the purpose of carrying on the practice. Galbraith was appointed Chief Engineer to the LSWR and Tolme assisted on other projects around the country, including the Mid-Hants Railway. When the partnership was dissolved in 1869, he continued on other works, including the Metropolitan District Railway's extension to Hammersmith and the Devil's Dyke railway, north of Brighton. Tolme died from acute rheumatism at the age of 42 on 25th December 1878 and was buried at Highgate Cemetery in London.

At the first General Meeting of the A,A&WR Co held at the Swan Hotel in December 1861, and with Errington still as engineer, the Chairman, Edward Knight, stated that he, "trusted that the line was now being staked out, or at the latest, that the engineer would commence doing so this week". Errington's poor health probably meant that Tolme did much of this work under his direction and of course took over completely the task of engineer-in-charge in July 1862.

More problems confronted the Directors; shares in the scheme were not taken up as generally as had been hoped, despite great exertions on the part of the Directors. Only about £20,000 had been subscribed, although some local landowners had agreed to take shares in payment for some of their land which was required for construction. Others also agreed to lease their land to the Company to save on the initial expense of buying it outright (some of these arrangements exist today!). The Chairman himself was willing to sell the 18 ½ acres of his land for £2,000, half in shares and half in cash, to be paid within one year of the commencement of construction.

There was clearly insufficient capital in the bank to build the line with an estimate cost of £150,000. Then, on 4th August 1862, the Board received a letter from a Mr Arthur Hankey offering to finance the construction within three years for "certain financial considerations". This offer was discussed at the half-yearly meeting on Monday 25th August and a resolution passed to confirm the arrangements made by the Directors. The Board were, however, in some doubt as to the legality of the proposed arrangement with Hankey and sought opinion from Arthur Kekewich, an eminent lawyer. His opinion, in a letter dated 18th September 1862, said that it was a perfectly legal arrangement. Despite this, further doubts were still expressed and a second opinion sought. In the meantime another letter was received by the Board from Arthur Hankey asking why the resolution carried at the meeting on 25th August had not been actioned. He asked for a meeting at which matters could be resolved and this was called for the 8th or 9th October.

At some point Hankey entered into a partnership with a Benjamin Bateman (who later became a Director) for the purpose of financing the railway's construction.

Hankey knew that the Company could not raise sufficient capital and was therefore willing to get involved, at a price! The arrangement was to involve the use of Lloyds Bonds. These were nothing to do with Lloyds Bank and would be redeemed later on for shares in the Company. The Bonds were invented by one John Horatio Lloyd and were securities under the seal of the Company to the party in whose favour they were executed, with a covenant to pay a sum of money, with interest.

These bonds were not popular with shareholders because they were negotiable only at a high rate of discount, something taken into account by the person making the contract with the company. Thus the cost of any work financed by this arrangement would be more than if the company had sufficient share capital. Yet it is true to say that the arrangement was voted for by the shareholders of the A,A&WR Co at its General Meeting. They had little choice if the railway was to be built.

Arthur Hankey wrote his letters from Whittington Hall, near Chesterfield, Derbyshire. He did not actually live there but was most likely staying as a guest of William Fowler, the brother of John Fowler, the well-known railway engineer. It is highly interesting that Hankey, referred to as a banker, must have known John Fowler. He (Fowler) had been

Above: This extraordinary view of Alresford was taken around construction period, certainly before 1873 as the grain store is not in place. The bridge is that carrying Sun Lane over the line. The main station buildings are in place, having been constructed by Bull & Sons, a local company. The very steep embankments are noticeable and already look as though they have deteriorated. *Winchester Museums Service* *Below:* This is the main Winchester to Alton road at Four Marks circa 1905, forty years after the railway arrived. The post office on the left is now a private house. The journey by rail must have been preferable to that by road! *Edward Roberts collection*

The line just after building in the Ashdell area to the south of Alton. The bridge became known as Ashdell bridge.

Hampshire County Museum's Service

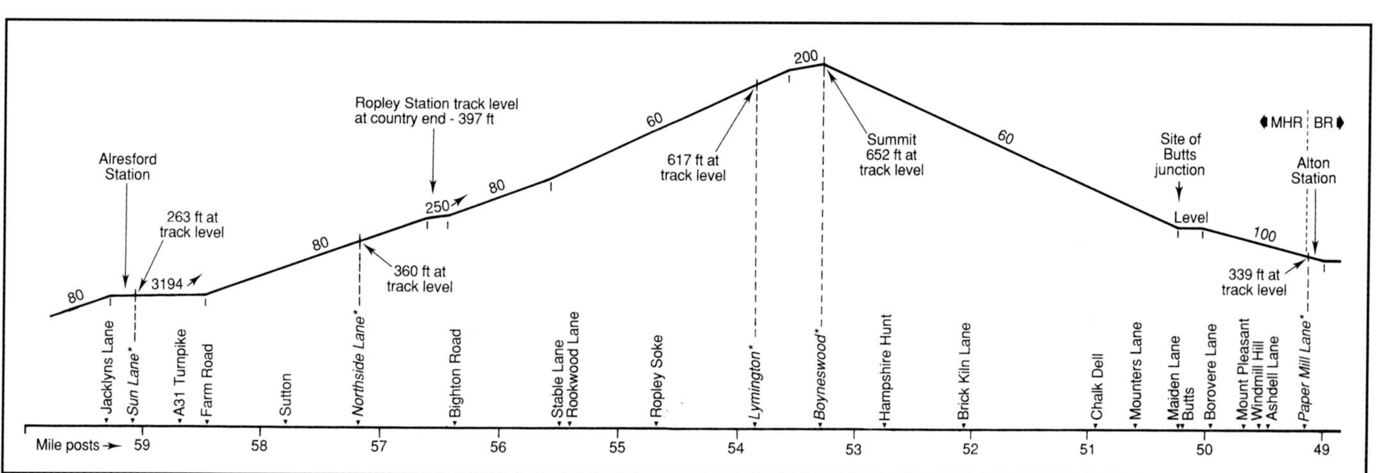

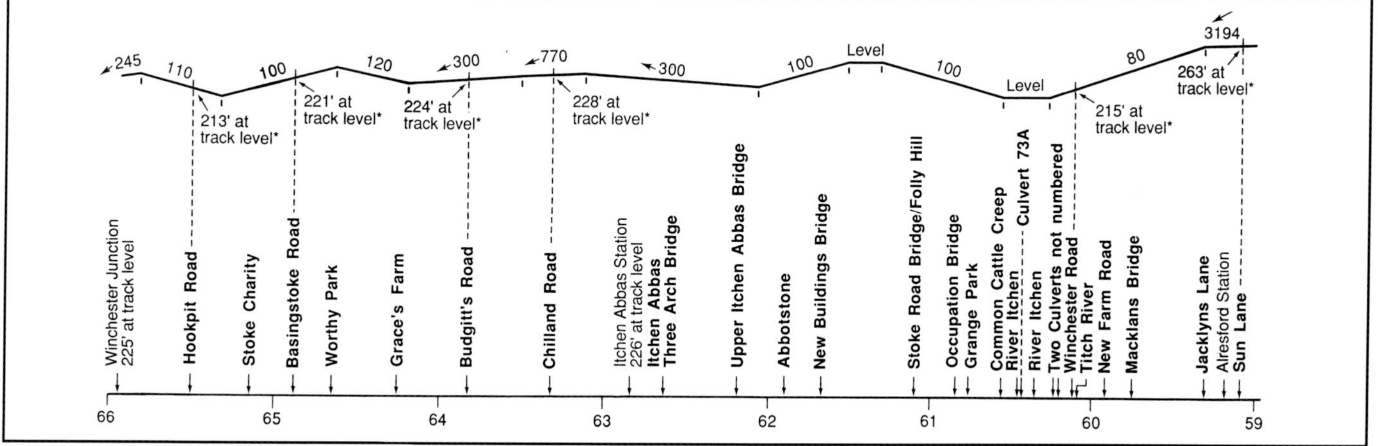

Gradient profiles of the railway, from Alton to Alresford and from Alresford to Winchester Junction. *Courtesy John Elliott*

engineer to the Metropolitan Railway in London, which opened in January 1863. He had used the contracting firm of Smith & Knight and they, having completed the works there, must have been looking for new contracts. Hankey entered into a contract to finance the building of the A,A&WR on 3rd February 1863 and used Smith & Knight as contractors, surely more than a co-incidence.

Smith & Knight started work about the second week in February 1863, perhaps using some of the workmen involved in the Metropolitan Railway. George Porter, Secretary of the A,A&WR Co, had communicated with Hankey's partner, Benjamin Bateman, on 4th February, at which time Bateman said that earthworks would be vigorously commenced almost immediately.

Smith & Knight's responsibility was to fence off the course of the line, excavate the cuttings and use the spoil from these to build the embankments. The 22 under bridges and 20 over bridges would also be built. Priority was given to the section from Alton to Alresford, with the hope of opening this part by the autumn of 1864. Much of the land was owned by Edward Knight and so this could be worked upon with a degree of ease and cost. However, it was thought that completion of the Windmill Hill cutting would ultimately determine the time at which the line would be ready for opening. Total expenditure by the Company up to 30th June 1863 was £19,750, with a maximum input by the contractors of 400 men and 30 horses. The line eastwards from Winchester Junction had been started for a length of about two miles by this time, but from here to Alresford much of the land was still to be purchased.

By 31st December 1864 total expenditure was £71,651, reflecting much progress by Smith & Knight. By this time works were in hand throughout almost the whole line of railway, leaving just a few parcels of land to be purchased and worked upon.

Living conditions for the navvies who built the line were fairly primitive. Some lived in huts whose walls were constructed of turf, wood, brick or stone, with roofs of tiles or tarpaulines. These encampments were at various points along the line and one had a reasonably permanent church constructed nearby. A more well-known building, referred to as 'The Shant', eventually appeared by the main Winchester to Alton road, now known as the A31. This was sited quite close to the line and still survives at the time of writing as a kitchen showroom.

Sadly the work was not completed without accident. On 1st October 1864, Robert Taylor, a 21 year old labourer, was employed on the works of the new railway. The *Hampshire Chronicle* of 8th October 1864 reported, "he was at work at Bishop's Sutton, where at seven o'clock in the morning he was employed picking with some other labourers, whilst another lot of men were 'barring' some three tons of chalk about nine feet above him. One of his fellow labourers saw an opening in the chalk above and warned the deceased to get out of the way, as the 'muck' was coming down. He did not heed the friendly warning, but said 'there is no danger' and continued his work. Almost immediately afterwards the whole mass came tumbling down, struck the deceased on the back and a huge block rolling away struck his head and kept it down upon the rails. The lump was removed and the wounded man, still sensible, called upon those about him to pull him out, which was immediately done, when it became evident that serious injury had been inflicted. He was carried to his lodgings and a medical attendant was at once procured. He advised removal to the hospital and thither deceased was conveyed in a fly. Everything was done to relieve him, but he died about five o'clock on Tuesday morning. A post-mortem examination showed that rupture of the bladder was the proximate cause of death, resulting from the serious injuries received. Verdict: Accidental death".

January 1865 was an unhappy month for the railway, its workers and in one case the wife of a labourer. Sarah Pearce was buried on 2nd January 1865. Along with her husband, she had lived in a hut made of bricks and sand close to the site of the railway bridge then about to be started at Itchen Stoke. The hut had no window and Sarah had been ill before they moved in. After living in the hut for only a few weeks, she became much worse and was taken to hospital in Winchester. She was described as being in a wretched and filthy state and covered in vermin. The hospital sent her away and she was then taken to Alresford Union Workhouse, but died that night. A furious correspondence followed in the *Hampshire Chronicle* with accusations being made that the hospital should not have turned her away and that her life might otherwise have been saved. But the hospital stated that they were not obliged to, "take in vagrants" and stressed the filthy state she was in.

On 20th January of the same year, the railway had what must have been its saddest day. That evening, between six and seven o'clock, a deplorable accident resulting in the loss of three lives, occurred in the parish of Ropley. Eleven men were engaged in removing earth from a cutting about 15 feet deep, when a sudden slip of earth occurred, burying seven of the unfortunate men. Four were pulled out injured but alive, the other three were dead at the time they were reached. The funerals took place on Monday

Springvale Bridge, the last bridge structure before the line joins the main line at Winchester Junction. This construction period photograph captures a group of workers poised directly above the bridge arch. A contractor's locomotive is in view. In October 1864, Mr Tolme, the MHR engineer, requested that a locomotive's tyres be turned at the Nine Elms works of the LSWR. The LSWR agreed to this providing the contractor paid for the expense. *Winchester Museums Service*

afternoon 23rd January 1865 at Ropley, in the presence of hundreds of spectators. All three were buried in the same grave. The whole of the labourers on the line were given time off to attend. The inquest upon John Pomroy aged 25 from Taunton, James Edwards aged 28 and John Smith aged 22, heard evidence from fellow labourers William Bell and John Miller. James Cooper, a representative of the sub-contractors and Edward Harrison, referred to as 'manager of the line', also appeared before the coroner.

The following month, in February 1865, saw public protests about the contractor who was working on the line on Sundays. A memorial was presented to the Directors of the railway company at the February half-yearly meeting and they agreed to communicate it to Smith & Knight. The Directors were even prepared to authorise the county police to patrol the line and pay expenses of any subsequent local prosecutions. The same Board Meeting expressed hope that the line would be open in time for summer traffic. Once the main earthworks and track laying were sufficiently advanced, work could begin on the stations and these were built by the firm of Bull & Sons, thought to originate in Southampton. A tank was supplied by Lloyds Foster and all the signalling was supplied and installed by Stevens & Sons, the LSWR's main contractor for this important part of the railway infrastructure.

On 12th July 1865, the Secretary of the Mid-Hants Railway Company wrote to the Committee of Privy Council for Trade, giving one month's notice of their intention to open the railway, but this proved to be premature. The *Hampshire Chronicle* for 26th August 1865 stated that the Directors were making arrangements for the line to be opened on 11th September, but with the rider that further delay might be caused by the LSWR, who were superintending the new station arrangements at Alton (they had only purchased some land required for the new station at Alton in January of that year!).

The Company again wrote to the Committee of Privy Council for Trade on 12th September, giving ten days notice for inspection. It was stated that the Mid-Hants Engineer (Mr Tolme) and LSWR Traffic Manager would accompany the inspector through the line.

And so the railway was prepared for opening.

Chapter Two

The Route Described

The Mid-Hants Railway ran through some of the most spectacular countryside in southern England and 'called' into some delightful villages en route between Alton and Winchester.

If we look at this route which extended some 17 miles between the market town of Alton in the north east of Hampshire and the capital of the county at Winchester, we experience differing topography, from the higher chalk downs in the north to the more delicate meadowlands around Alresford and the Winchester downs of the southern section.

Alton

Alton was the largest town actually on the line. With a population of around 4,000 when the railway arrived, it more than equalled the rest of the line's residents put together. (The City of Winchester is not actually on the line, but had a population of 16,366 in 1875.) Apart from being an important market town, Alton was a centre for brewing, Crowley and Halls breweries forming a crucial local industry.

Since 1852 the town had a railway link from the north which was a fast way for the breweries to get their ales to London and when a map of the area is consulted, it was only natural for the line to be extended in some direction southwards.

Alton became a railhead out of the scheme to build a line from Guildford via Farnham through an Act of Parliament in 1846, these being the very beginnings of the future Mid-Hants line. The Act stated: "The Line to finish in a 'field' in the parish of Alton in the County of Southampton, belonging to Mr Henry Hall (also proprietor of Hall's brewery off Lower Turk Street) and abutting to the public road leading to Worldham". Mr Hall's name would surface again when the Alton, Alresford & Winchester Railway Company was formed fifteen years later.

In fact things became quite drawn out and the LSWR had to ask for an extension of the three year period to build the line. When Captain Laffans of the Board of Trade inspected the route in August 1849 he deemed the line to Ash was worthy of operation, but that to Farnham was incomplete with "shifting rails and unfinished platforms". Eventually all was ready to Farnham at least, and this section opened on 8th

A view of Alton from Windmill Hill at around the time just after construction of the railway. The line is seen in the foreground with several men seemingly working on replacing sleepers, perhaps at the insistence of the Board of Trade Inspector. Alton's population was just 4,000 at this time. *Hampshire County Museum's Service*

October 1849. The remaining 8 ¾ miles to Alton had to wait a further three years before opening. On 21st July 1852 Captain D. Galton, Royal Engineers, of the Board of Trade, commented that he, "sanctioned the single line from Farnham to Alton for opening if the signalling and fencing was completed and a careful watch given to the landslip hazard". He also stated, "an engine turntable is to be erected at Alton station to preclude the necessity of tender foremost as is the case between Farnham and Guildford".

Alton received its first train seven days later. At the time of opening, Alton's station building was a very impressive stone-built structure which actually survived until the 1960s. It would be a terminus until 1865, when the Mid-Hants line opened, with considerable rebuilding in the vicinity to enable a realignment to take the line southwards towards Winchester. Quite an extensive goods yard developed north of the station which, by 1896, had six sidings running off the 'main line' close to the old Workhouse, with a further three south of the line, one of which incorporated the turntable. The 1865 station building was very unlike the 1852 version, being just a single storey building with a canopy at the entrance. There was a proposal for a subway at the station to connect the 'up' and 'down' platforms in 1884 but this was rejected. However, in December 1891, the General Manager of the LSWR, Sir Charles Scotter, approved a footbridge, which was covered in during 1894 and glazed in 1896 at a cost of £170!

All Change At Alton

A further major change was to take place at Alton in the late 1890s when, in 1897, two new lines were proposed. The first, to run from the town along the Mid-Hants line and turn south towards Fareham at the Butts (the Meon Valley Railway) and another following the same course to the Butts, but turning to the north (the Basingstoke & Alton Light Railway). Construction of the Meon Valley line started in differing locations in 1898 and in January 1899 the then Board of Trade Inspector, Sir F. Marindin, sanctioned for the contractors' use a temporary spur off the Mid-Hants line at Butts to facilitate access. This was sited east of the Butts bridge and formed a crossover with a short stretch of double line with the Mid-Hants line. A similar agreement was made in August 1899 for the contractors on the Basingstoke & Alton; this junction was sited where the line was eventually to run from. Both lines were operated by a ground frame with six levers sited east of the Butts bridge and locked by a key from the Alton signalbox.

At this time there was no sight of the double line from Alton or the signalbox at the Butts.

The two new lines heralded the start of a widening programme between Farnham and the new Butts Junction. The new 8 mile 16 chain section from Farnham to Alton became the 'up' line and was nearly ready for opening by May 1900. The new

Alton station looking towards London, prior to the First World War. This photograph was taken after the Meon Valley line had begun services in 1903, as the 'down' platform is now an island one. The train ready to depart is a service for Gosport and will go down the Meon Valley with the 'T9' Class at the helm. The LSWR approved the building of the new 'down' line and new sidings and accommodation in December 1902, costing some £6288. *Author's collection*

Above: A particularly good view of the station area at Alton with the new buildings of 1865 on the right and the original building on the left. The photographer is positioned roughly in line with the old track which was a terminus point. *R.W. Small collection*

Left: A close-up of the old 1852 building, how elegant it was. When the new station was built, this building was divided into two houses, one for the stationmaster and one for the line inspector. In 1859 James Richardson was stationmaster; his son, George, later became a Senior Clerk. A Mr Tracy was an early stationmaster at Alton, he was very religious and held weekly open air 'services' in the station yard for many years until his retirement. *Author's collection*

section from Alton to the Butts, forming the 'down' line, was sanctioned for provisional use by the end of May 1901, in time for when the Basingstoke line was opened for use on 1st June. It would be a further two years before the Meon Valley line opened. Major Pringle's inspection for the Board of Trade on 21st May 1901 outlined some alterations at Alton station: "The signalbox has been lengthened to carry more levers to control the double line. The signalbox at Butts is new and will form a new block post". He also commented that the siding to the Cripples Home had not been completed; it was to be a further nine years before this opened. There were new crossover points at each end of the through lines.

Further changes took place at Alton station in early 1903 to cope with the new Meon Valley services; the 'down' platform became an island one with a new Platform 3 being created. The old 'down' line became the 'up' loop line and a siding was installed adjacent to the new Platform 3 line. Both platforms were extended, the one at Platform 1 in the northerly direction incorporating the signalbox. The Secretary of the LSWR, Mr George Knight, asked the BoT for an inspection of the new layout on 18th May 1903: "We are anxious to benefit from improved accommodation in connection with the opening of the Meon line".

A Journey Along the Mid-Hants Railway

We will now take a journey down the line to Winchester Junction as seen at the time of the opening in 1865. The new Mid-Hants Railway runs just to the south-east of the old original line and Alton terminus station, forming a through route. On departure from Platform 2 (the 'down' side) at the station, the line almost immediately crosses Paper Mill Lane, the first of fifty-eight bridges and culverts on the entire route. Travelling in a south-westerly direction and on a

Above: The scene at Butts junction circa 1900/1. Contractor's locomotives building the Meon Valley railway use the temporary piece of line which joined the MHR behind the camera. The Basingstoke & Alton line is not yet open, but the junction is in place. The new signalbox would shortly be built at the furthest end of the parapet of Bridge No. 52. *Below:* Men work on the construction of the new 'down' line and embankment close to Borovere Lane Bridge. This section from Alton was fully opened in time for trains starting on the Basingstoke line in May 1901. The MHR line on the far side had been open some 35 years by this time and became the 'up' line for all trains. *Both,David Foster-Smith collection*

Above: The brewery siding at Alton in 1905, the earliest known view. The buildings are those belonging to Crowley's brewery, the ones owned by Mr Henry Hall (bought out by Courage's in 1903) are visible behind these on the other side of Lower Turk Street. A series of sidings went off the main one and several wagon turntables were used around the brewery to turn vehicles as required.

Below: Main line locomotives did not enter the siding and the workings were the responsibility of the owners. This little diesel engine arrived in July 1935 and was built by Hunslet at Leeds. It was one of only two that were used throughout the duration of the siding's use and had a 20 hp Lister engine capable of speeds up to seven miles per hour! (Since being taken out of use, it has been preserved on the Middleton Railway, at Leeds.) Crowley's had been brewers since 1763 in Alton and Henry Hall had come from Ely, Cambridgeshire in 1847. The siding was not used after 1968.

Both, Geoff Dye collection

A photograph taken on 27th March 1952 looking towards Alton with 'M7' Class No. 30081. Note the brewery siding in the far distance on the left and the steel sleepers of the Meon Valley line. *D.Clayton*

Above: A familiar view of an early Meon Valley line train as it arrives at Butts Junction. Stovepipe chimneyed 'F6' Class No. 362 was built in 1896, so it was not very old when this photograph was taken, shortly after the Meon Valley line opened in 1903. An embankment of the Basingstoke & Alton line can be seen swinging in on the right. The photographer is standing roughly on the spot where a platform was built for the exchange of 'down' single line tablets for all three lines. There are stories of the tablet being dropped over the side of the embankment on occasions! *The late E.C. Griffith collection*

slight embankment, the paper mill itself is passed on the left with the River Wey quite close by at this point. The line becomes single from here on, although all the bridges and course of track are built to double track width at the insistence of the LSWR.

Curving slightly to the right and entering a cutting the line crosses over the River Wey and Ash Dell Lane. Before going under Windmill Hill bridge, the siding is passed on the right which runs into the premises of Crowley & Company and Halls the brewers. (This was built in the 1880s and had up to four other sidings off the main one. In 1905 the LSWR agreed to take on the maintenance of these sidings although Messrs Crowley and Courage (Hall's had sold out in 1903) had to pay for improvement costs of £630 before this maintenance agreement came into being.) Rising on a gradient of 1 in 100 another cutting is ahead and the 3-arched over bridge of Mount Pleasant is seen aloft. A further 24 chains and we go under Borovere Lane bridge.

We are now within sight of the Butts under bridge and 1 mile 3.7 chains from Alton station. This bridge was originally of wooden construction and was renewed in 1900 out of wrought iron when the line was doubled as far as this point for the Meon Valley and Basingstoke lines. Almost immediately the line crosses Maiden Lane and rises steeply towards Medstead station on an embankment and at the start of an incline of 1 in 60. This is the section that gave the railway the nickname of 'over the Alps' and as we shall see later, it caused enginemen many difficulties over the years. Mounters Lane and Chalk Dell bridge's are crossed before we go over No. 55, Brick Kiln Lane bridge and into a cutting again which deepens as we climb to the summit. We have now climbed approximately 200 feet since leaving Alton. This cutting is one of many along the 17 mile line cut through the chalk-based remnants of the South Downs and has very steeply graded sides to it.

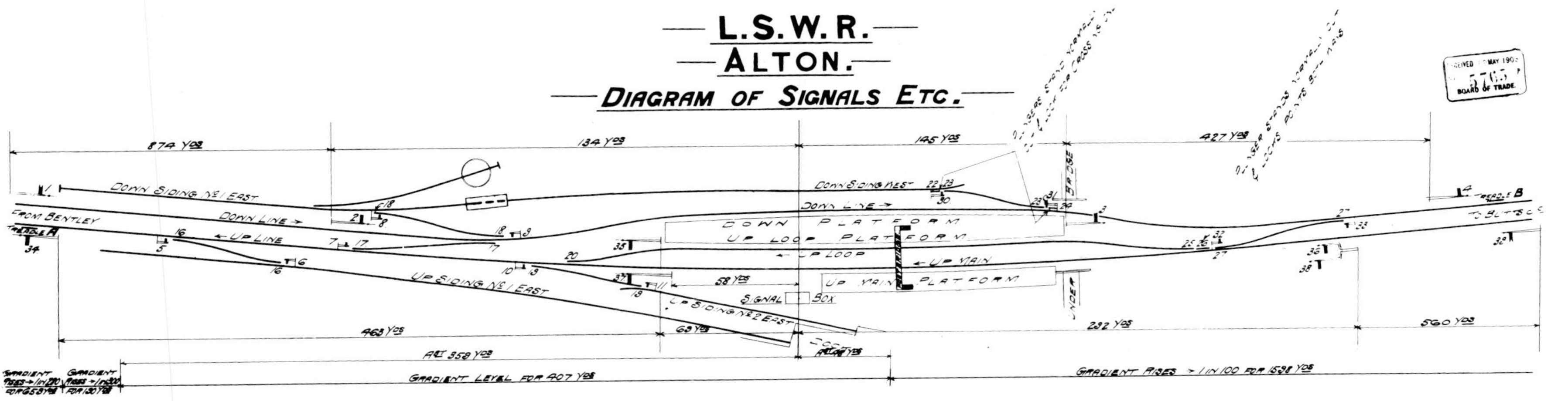

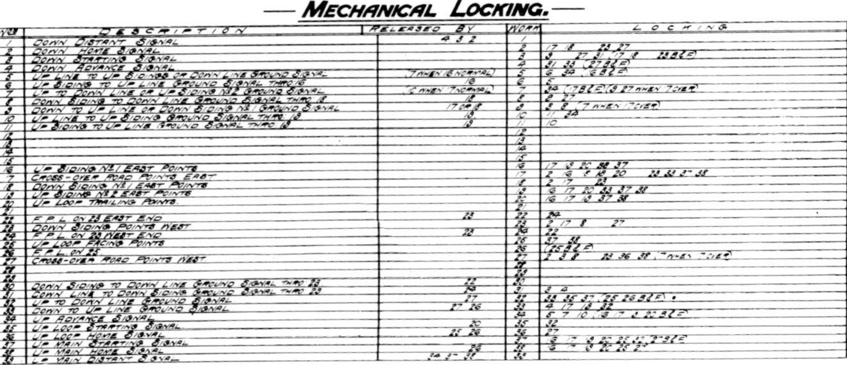

Above: A new diagram of signals at Alton as sent to the Board of Trade in May 1903. The track layouts involved in the re-organisation of the station for the soon-to-be-opened Meon Valley line are to be noted. *Left:* Alton's signalbox lever frame as photographed in March 1972. At this time the section was between Alton and Alresford, but from 1901 until 1935 the section would have been through to Butts Junction signalbox. On removal of this box in 1935 the section was then between Alton and Medstead. *Right:* A close-up of the frame levers showing those dedicated to Mid-Hants functions in 1972. No. 39 has been pulled out of sight for an 'up' train. On 19th December 1935 the 10.04am Waterloo to Gosport train locomotive was handed the incorrect tablet, that for Medstead. A taxi had to be called for its collection at Tisted,

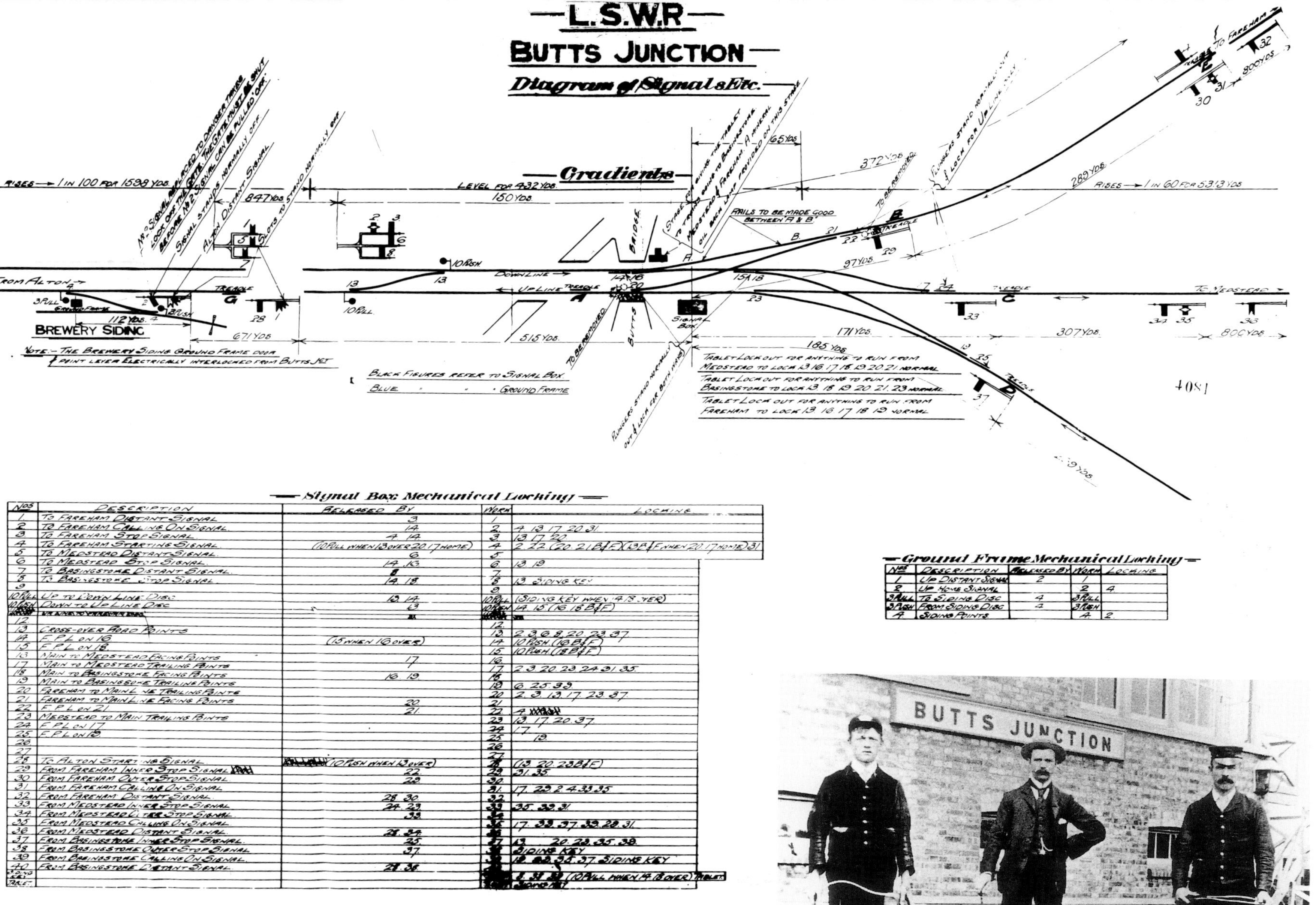

Above: The signalling diagram supplied in April 1903 in conjunction with the inspection by the Board of Trade of the Meon Valley line. *Right:* A rare look at the outside of Butts Junction signalbox circa 1904/5. Those in view are thought to be from left to right; signalbox lad, signal engineer and signalman. Both the lad and signalman have a single line token pouch in their hands. This would contain a token for transfer to the engine crew as they passed.

Ron Neal collection

Left: An even more interesting view of the interior of the box, at around the same date. From the levers pulled, it would seem that a Mid-Hants train has just passed by towards Medstead and that the road for an 'up' passage from the Meon Valley is set. Note the three Tyers No.6 token instruments to the right of the signalman's hand, one for each of the three line's in his control and the spare pouches hanging up behind him. From the opening of the box until its closure, the single line section was from Alton to Butts and from Butts to Medstead. The signalman's hand is placed on the No. 10 lever, a push-pull one, seen at its normal position. This controlled the crossover signals, pulling for a 'down' movement and pushing for an 'up' movement. When the Basingstoke & Alton line finally closed in 1933, the layout at Butts was simplified, with the Meon Valley having its own dedicated line without any junction to the Mid-Hants and the line to Medstead operated solely on the old 'up' line. This left the signalbox at Butts redundant and it was finally closed in February 1935.

R Neal collection

Above: Keeping on a signalling theme, here is the only known view of the interior of Ropley signalbox. It is dated around 1930, just a few months before the box was dispensed with, in September 1931. The railwayman posing in this unique photograph is Mr Harry White, who spent four years working at Ropley until made redundant in 1931 and moving on to another post.

Mrs A. E. Colliver (nee White) collection

In very much a country setting, this photograph shows us Medstead station at the turn of the century and well before it was renamed Medstead & Four Marks in 1937. The 'up' side goods yard is in view. The large house on the right was the stationmaster's residence. Mr F. Benians recalls how his father, who had arrived to grow roses and fruit trees in the area during the early part of the century, used the telegraph office at the station. *Lens of Sutton*

Medstead

The line and cutting turns to the right and then to the left at which point a narrow footpath bridge is passed under (this was later rented by the Hampshire Hunt Club in 1937 for £1 per annum and became known as the Hampshire Hunt Bridge). Track then passes beneath the high structure of the three-arched Boyneswood Road bridge. At approximately 650 feet above sea level the station at Medstead is ahead of us. To quote Captain Tyler, the Board of Trade Inspector of the line before opening, he stated in his report of 30th September 1865 that: "At Medstead, which is 4 ½ miles from Alton, a passenger platform has been constructed, but it is not at present, I understand, intended to use it for passengers. If at any time it was worked as a crossing place, a loop line and second platform would be required".

Medstead station is the odd one out as it was not built prior to the line opening, the local residents having to wait until August 1868 before they could join others in the area for a trip by train. The station buildings were single-storeyed and very basic, the stationmaster's house by far the most impressive structure. The stationmaster, or 'agent' at that time was a Mr Grimbley; certainly he was there from September 1871 as he was awarded 20 shillings by the LSWR for discovering a broken wheel on a goods wagon on that date. He won another 20 shillings three years later for repairing a telegraph wire, so he was supplementing his wages of around £100 per year quite well! Mr Grimbley was a figure of Medstead until he moved on to Cobham in December 1884.

A siding was installed at Medstead known as Hutchings Siding (it ceased to be used in the early 1930s) and a cattle loading bank built in 1873. In 1878 it was requested that a shelter be erected on the 'down' side and this was built in the following year at a cost of £70. Later, in October 1883, approval was given to lengthen the siding and install a 30 cwt crane; a 'wash house' was also built at the Agent's house. Shortly after this, a Mr Arthur Scott asked for a siding on the 'down' side, but this was not sanctioned, although he was told if he wanted one, he had to pay for it.

The next major step in the life of the station came in 1897 when the General Manager, Sir Charles Scotter, put forward a scheme to lengthen the loop line and platforms. He said that if old sleepers were used instead of bricks for the platform, the whole work would cost £390. This was declined in committee stage at Waterloo and would be raised again in 1901 following an accident in 1900 which had dramatic consequences. (See Accidents chapter.)

It was agreed to provide the extended loop and platforms in March 1901 at a cost now of £430! Major Pringle carried out the inspection of the completed works on 8th November 1901: "The loop line has been lengthened at Medstead by 125 yards at the south west end. Balance weight catch points inserted on the

Medstead was not characteristic of the other stations on the line, possibly due to the financial state of the company at the time it was built. There are plans that exist which show the station building was going to have a canopy added, but this never happened. Note the ballast which looks to be in poor condition and the form of topiary on the platform. It would be 1924 before a telephone line was installed at the station, initially costing £1 15s per quarter. *Lens of Sutton*

'up' loop ascending line, to act as a trap for runaways down the 1 in 60. Being over 200 yards from the signalbox, points are worked from a new ground frame at the south western end of the 'down' platform. The frame in the signalbox has 15 levers, 3 of which are spare, one is a push-pull lever. All done in consequence of an accident in 1900 when a horsebox ran away. Lamp Room moved to station yard 'up' side". These new works would be tested to the full twice in 1915 (see Accidents chapter).

There was some vehicular access to the station across the line at the southern end and the Engineering Department requested in May 1901 that this be closed, although a key was given to a Mr M. Knight and Mr F. Nash. It would be a further 36 years before the name was adopted as Medstead & Four Marks, pretty amazing as the station was so close to Four Marks itself.

We now resume our journey after reaching the summit of the line at Medstead station and leave the way we came in, this time down at 1 in 60!

The line enters a shallow cutting and then opens out onto an embankment to cross over the large Lymington Bottom Road bridge. A deep cutting is then entered before the railway opens out onto a high embankment and over the tunnel-like Ropley Soke bridge. The line now clings onto the hillside for most of its path to Ropley and beyond in fact. Three more bridges are encountered (Rookwood Lane, Stable Lane and Bighton Road) before the easing 1 in 80 gradient brings us into Ropley station, 397 feet above sea level.

Ropley

Captain Tyler in his report on 30th September 1865, three days before opening, said: "As the gradient west of Ropley is at 1 in 80, I have recommended that the loop line be extended 100 yards further west and a pair of catch points installed on the 'up' line as a safeguard against vehicles running back upon that line". Regarding the track itself on the whole line he commented, " the rails are of 75 lbs at 24 feet in length. The ballast is of such material as could be purchased on the line - a mixture of chalk, flint and gravel. I recommend that the chairs are not of a standard capable of high speeds or heavy trains and need replacing".

The station site was a good distance from the village of Ropley, the residents of which, on foot, had to walk on a footpath, across the main Winchester to Alton road and up another footpath through a field to a point near Bighton Road bridge which took them into the station yard. Passengers would then pass three sidings situated to the north of the station, which were extensively used by local merchants and

Above: Quite possibly the best photograph of the railway showing all aspects of life at Ropley before the station house was rebuilt with the additional bedroom in 1894. Mr Anderson, who was appointed station Agent in 1892, is on the far right on the platform with porter/signalman Roberts, a clerk, porter/signalman Windybank, others unknown, then Mr Newman (with foot on rail) and Bill Connors. The station was very cut off from Ropley itself, with just the large Ropley Lodge building to the south-west the only one nearby. There was a path from this house to the station. *Below:* An equally interesting photograph, but of not such good quality, looking south towards Alresford; the lamp room, goods store and station buildings from left to right. Note the 'pillar' or 'flap' signal for the siding. *MHR Archives*

Above: Another view looking towards Alton, the sidings and loading platform are visible at Ropley. By now the new room has been added to the station building. If the MHR Co's plans of 1864 had succeeded, another line running to the south through a field owned by Mr Jacob Lagan would have made Ropley a Junction. *Lens of Sutton*

Left: This was taken after the ground frame was put in to control the siding and just before the signalbox was removed in 1931. Note the nice lamp on the side of the signalbox. All lamps on the station at this time were fuelled by oil. *Mrs A. E. Colliver*

Below: Ropley was a Class 5 station under the LSWR. Here we see another portrait of the staff, certainly prior to the loop going in 1931. A Mr W. H. Wray was appointed stationmaster in April 1923 at £200 per annum. *MHR Archives*

farms. These were known as the Long Siding and Dock Road and a shorter siding running back off the Long siding. The short siding was added in September 1872. The Long siding had a raised platform for the loading of horses, the carriage of these animals being quite extensive in those days. Coal was another crucial commodity carried by rail and Ropley was no exception, having an area for coal storage south of the signalbox and short siding.

The station itself comprises a single storey booking office with a stationmaster's house attached, which is a two storeyed building with a lean-to. These are on the 'down' side. To the north of the buildings are a goods store (erected in 1879 at a cost of £40) and lamp room together with the signalbox. In August 1894 approval was given (at a cost of £90) for a further bedroom at the house and so the building took on quite a different appearance after that.

There was a garden for the stationmaster in two parts of the station area, firstly on the 'up' side platform, behind the waiting shelter and secondly in an area on the other side of the approach road, directly opposite the house.

Ropley is surely best known for its incredible topiary work. This was started quite early on in the station's life and was a tradition carried on through to closure. This particular tree was close to the goods store and the side gate. Mr Harry White is shown clipping the tree. He was employed at Ropley between 1926 and 1931, leaving after the loop and signalbox was removed. The 1931 photograph also gives us a rare view of the 'up' platform waiting shelter. *Mrs A.E. Colliver (nee White) collection*

Perhaps the most noticeable aspect, however, about Ropley is its elegant topiary on the 'down' platform. As many as eight or nine of these beautifully 'carved' trees were in view from an early time and were a credit to the staff of the station over the years.

In the 1870s records of Junior Clerks were as follows: Mr W. C. Wilson appointed 6th April 1871; Mr John Tate in January 1872; Mr W. Smith in 1873; Mr H. Hall appointed on 15th January 1874. The Agent in 1892, Mr W. J. Anderson, was awarded a salary increase in that year taking it to £90 a year.

Following a Directors' visit over the line in 1897, the LSWR's General Manager proposed that the 'up' platform be extended. This was approved and cost some £210. From Ropley station, which is sited on an incline of 1 in 250, the line resumes a steep 1 in 80 gradient down towards Alresford, our next station. There are four road bridges on the section between Ropley and Alresford; Northside Lane, Sutton, the A31 Turnpike and Sun Lane, just prior to entering the station. There are also four culverts and one footpath underbridge on this stretch.

The railway is still hugging the chalk downs for the three miles a little way short of the Turnpike bridge opening out onto an embankment giving a good view of the countryside to the south and the luscious watercress beds, so important to the area's economy.

The gradient now virtually disappears for the approach to Alresford. As the A31 is crossed the line enters one of the steepest cuttings on the route, which contributed to the 1,300,000 cubic yards of earthworks in the construction period.

Alresford

Our journey now brings us to the main town served on the new section of railway - Alresford.

Four centuries before the railway arrived, Alresford was in the top ten in England for its wool trade, and was the third richest town in Hampshire.

Above: West Street, Alresford looking towards the west and Winchester. The sign for the Swan Hotel can just be seen on the left. This hotel was often the meeting place for the directors of the Mid-Hants Railway Company and also marks the corner of Station Road. *Edward Roberts collection* *Below:* A winter-time photograph of Alresford looking north, which allows views of the station goods yard. This view was taken before 1906. The proposed new scheme by the MHR for a railway south towards Bishop's Waltham from Ropley was then switched to run from a point close to Jacklyn's bridge and go southwards via Cheriton and through parishes towards Exton. Needless to say nothing became of the idea. *MHR Archives*

A panoramic view of the town from the then new water tower erected off Jacklyn's Lane circa 1910. St. John's church and the police house are in view and the station looks as though it is very much in the country. The sidings to the goods yard ran off the 'up' loop line close to the goods shed and the feeder line came back towards Itchen Abbas about one hundred yards over Jacklyn's bridge. Wagons with 'Foster & Co.' are in the coal siding at the left-centre of the photograph and others with 'LSWR' addorning their sides are in the goods shed and grain store sidings. One 'watercress' wagon is in the siding next to the latter. *Edward Roberts collection*

Fire seems to have been Alresford's main problem, with no fewer than seven major blazes, the worst in 1689 when the town was totally destroyed. New Alresford, by which name it is really known, was laid out by Bishop Godfrey de Lucy in around 1200AD and he quickly seized upon the opportunities given to Alresford by the nearby River Itchen. He made a dam on the town's River Arle to form a reservoir over some 200 acres as a means of keeping the River Itchen navigable to Southampton for the transportation of wool. The reservoir still remains, now called Old Alresford Pond, albeit in a smaller state.

Rodney's Railway

It is perhaps not widely known that Alresford had a railway twenty years before the Mid-Hants line appeared. Around the 1843 period Robert Dennett Rodney, grandson of the famous admiral, Lord Rodney, built his own railway in the field next to his home at Cardew House in East Street, New Alresford. This was a curious affair, it is reported, "in a circle of approximately ¾ mile round". The *Hampshire Chronicle* reported on 27th March 1843 that, "its course presents various specimens of engineering, including a tunnel 70 yards long under the trees by the side of the Alton Road. A locomotive and two beautifully finished coaches are being built for the line, which is expected to be opened for use soon after Easter". It is also reported by a local personality that the line took two and a half years to complete with sixty navvies employed. The name of the engine was *Formidable*. The gauge of the track is not known, but there was a third rail for the operation of another smaller locomotive. It is not known how long the railway existed, but it certainly disappeared before the start of the twentieth century.

The 1861 census puts Alresford's population at 1,618 contained within 282 houses. Whites Directory of 1859 informs us that "there is a market every Thursday for corn etc and a fair four times a year for the sheep and cattle trade. The town has a bank, brewery and iron foundry. John Freeman's omnibus leaves the Swan daily at 9.30 am for Winchester. Collyer's London coach arrives from Southampton in time for breakfast at the Swan. The one from London arrives at 2pm on its way to Southampton".

Before the railway, the town was self sufficient in that it had its own court and solicitors, but these services moved to Winchester. In great anticipation of the railway coming, it was decided in August 1864 to

Above: The neat arrangement at Alresford station at the turn of the century. The waiting shelter on the 'down' platform is in place and the 1873 grain store, with its siding and three wagons. The gas lights are nicely arranged around the platforms. Note the signalman leaning out of his window; all signalboxes on the line later had their sides panelled over. *MHR Archives*

Below: The station looking from the church tower of St. John's, towards the south. The water tower on the western end of the 'down' platform is visible. This was removed in 1914 when the platform was extended. The police house dominates the foreground. After a burglary at the station in 1918, two soldiers were arrested by the local police. *Edward Roberts collection*

A view up Station Road towards the station. Pony and traps ply to and from the town. The police station is on the left and the Collis and Potters grain store right of the centre. The police house was replaced after the Second World War. It would be March 1926 before Alresford station was connected with a telephone at a cost of £7 p.a. *Edward Roberts collection*

build the Assembly Rooms in West Street and they were opened twelve days before the line during the September of 1865.

Alresford station was just over 59 miles from London and was sited in a comparatively rural location when built on the southern side of the town. One report suggests that the coming of the railway was the most important thing to happen to Alresford since the fire of 1736. This same source comments on the opening day of 2nd October 1865: "The first train from Alton into Alresford had two Alresford men on board, James Calvert, a director and owner of a drapery business in Broad Street and William Bulpitt, a banker".

On entering the station area by foot or alighting by train, a well laid out station building and yard with sidings were on view. Many locals found it easier to carry their luggage through St John's churchyard to catch the train as Station Road was very bumpey and difficult to negotiate. This was probably the most important station on the line, outside Alton, for traffic receipts and the legendary watercress trade began to use the railway for the transportation of their crops to London and much farther afield. It is perhaps with its watercress trade that Alresford is best known. The first reported commercially grown crops were in 1873 by a Mr Mills who came from Sussex to Bighton to start the process. The Alresford station goods rate book for 1896 shows that it cost 2s 0d per ½cwt of watercress for the journey to Waterloo and 3s 6d for the transfer to Birmingham. A spur off the siding near to the large grain store was often full of vans loading the fresh produce. This grain store dates from 1873 and is by far the largest building on the site. A Mr Collis, whose name together with a Mr Potter adorned the side of the building, asked the LSWR's Traffic Committee on 3rd April 1873 for a siding to his store being erected on his land. The reply was that he could have one if he paid for it, which he obviously did as it became a feature shortly afterwards. Later, in 1877, there was a proposal to extend the spur siding across the entrance to the station. However, this was declined, "as a level crossing across the public road would be against public safety".

The station building is very similar to that at Ropley, but it has a double fronted two-storeyed main building and lean-to on the eastern side. There is accommodation for the Agent (stationmaster) on the first floor with a kitchen, larder, scullery and space for coal on the ground floor. These buildings and a small office, the signalbox, goods shed and yard are on the 'up' side of the station. Three further sidings are in the yard to the south west of the station building, one serving the Dock, another to the goods shed and one to the coal yard. The whole area is fenced in with a very nice lattice-type wooden fencing.

In 1885 the station Agent asked for an office on the

Above: A view portraying the social and commercial aspects of the area around Alresford in 1917. The carts of watercress are loaded onto the vans for shipment to London and beyond. The cart on the left belonged to Mr Hunt of Fobdown Farm, the centre one to Mr Mills of Bishop's Sutton and the right-hand one is thought to belong to Mr Gill of Cheriton. *Mrs A. Colliver collection* *Below:* The staff circa 1918 pose with several vans in the background waiting to be loaded with watercress. Mr Knight was stationmaster at this time. Mr Ursell is on the far right and Mr Aslett who worked in the goods office is sitting in the centre. The LSWR uniform would comprise a red tie, black alpaca-sleeved waistcoat and dark green corduroy trousers.

Above: Looking towards Winchester. The grain store siding turns off to the right with its catch points visible. The tall lower quadrant starting signal, with its shunt arm half way down the post, dominates the end of the 'up' platform. The cattle-dock on the right was used a good deal by farmers locally who sent many sheep, particularly, by rail. *The late H.C. Casserley collection* *Below:* The station after a fall of snow. Note the porters room at the western end of the 'up' platform. *Lens of Sutton*

platform where brickwork had been built for a water tank . It is probable that this building is the one close to the signalbox, however, a water tank was situated just to the west of the 'down' platform virtually opposite the well which was close to the western edge of the main station buildings on the 'up' side. For a time there was also a porters' room at the western end of the 'up' platform.

The 'down' platform received its waiting shelter after an agreement by the Traffic Committee in July 1891 to spend £275 on its construction. In 1901 residents asked for longer platforms and a subway or footbridge and a path from the 'down' side to the road (Jacklyn's Lane). These requests were turned down, but in 1914 they got part of what they wanted in that the 'down' platform was extended by 98 feet and the loop line altered accordingly. The water tank was then demolished and a lamp room provided between the signalbox and the office. The passenger crossing at the western end was dispensed with as it was deemed that the one at the eastern end controlled passengers with more safety.

A plan does exist from November 1909 which proposed the extension of both platforms in an easterly direction. This would involve the cutting out of more chalk from both sides, the realignment of the siding and the abolition of the sleeper foot crossing. Joining the 400 foot-long platforms was a subway between the waiting shed on the 'down' side and the office on the 'up' side. Needless to say this scheme did not take place. With a salary of £100 a Mr Carter was the station agent in 1872. He would have had quite a staff of junior clerks and goods staff plus, of course, signalmen. This was a Class 4 station in LSWR days compared to Ropley, Medstead and Itchen Abbas which were classified Class 5. In January 1913 Mr G.E. Knight was appointed, at £230 per annum; he was there until his retirement in January 1926. Mr H. Newnham took over in February and also took charge of Ropley and Itchen Abbas from 11th April 1927.

Restarting our journey down the line we leave behind the sidings of Alresford and cross over the bridge at Jacklyn's Lane. The gradients from now on are less steep, although the first three quarters of a mile is down at 1 in 80 as the line progresses to Winchester Junction, 6 miles and 66 chains away to the west.

Very few photographs exist of the section of line between Alresford and Itchen Abbas and on to Winchester Junction. This view is at Itchen Stoke and is of 'M7' No. 30480 with a train from Alton to Eastleigh. The gradients on this section of the line were more in the region of 1 in 300 rather than 1 in 60! Ten days after the opening of the line, Mr Knight, the Chairman of MHR Co, on behalf of the Directors, requested passes from the LSWR to travel on the line. The LSWR declined, saying that they only owned the line and did not have any rights over it! *Peter Waylett*

A cutting is entered which runs behind Perin's school (named after Henry Perin who died in 1697) and then a road over bridge (Macklan's) is negotiated before the line passes under New Farm Road and turns to the right crossing the main road from Winchester. By now the line is on a high embankment and views are good from both sides of the carriage window. The rivers Arle and the Itchen are crossed; more watercress beds are to the south. Further cuttings are entered as we pass under Grange Park Road (an occupation bridge) and Stoke Road underbridges near Itchen Stoke. A look at the Ordnance Survey map shows us that we are now rounding the southern edge of Itchen Stoke Down and Folly Hill. Three more underbridges are negotiated at New Buildings Bridge, Abbotstone footpath and Upper Itchen Abbas as the line curves

A picture with a great deal of detail. This view of Itchen Abbas station is dated after 1891 as the additional bedroom has been added to the house. Very similar in layout to Ropley, although Itchen Abbas's signalbox was nearer to the main building. Note the dip in the platforms to allow foot access. The station formed an important link for the people of Avington.

Lens of Sutton

slightly to the left and over the largest bridge structure on the whole formation at Northington Road. We then enter the next and last station on the Mid-Hants Railway - Itchen Abbas.

Itchen Abbas

The layout at Itchen Abbas is very similar in every respect to that at Ropley, the station building having a single-storey office and waiting room and conveniences. The station house, attached, was originally a single two-storeyed affair with a lean-to, but had another bedroom built in 1891, making it a double two-storeyed building. As with Ropley, these buildings, the signalbox and goods yard are on the southern side of the line. It has a passing loop line and 'up' platform with waiting shelter. A distinctive 'dip' in both platforms lead to a foot crossing to give access. It all seems quite extensive for a location with very little population, but the farming community around quite clearly used the station for the carriage of their crops and cattle.

In 1870 a Mr Hodgson was the Agent at Itchen Abbas, although he was dismissed in February of that year for a late shipment. Junior clerks were; Mr C. Cooper appointed 4th May 1871; Mr John Blair appointed 8th February 1872; Mr Samuel Fay appointed 2nd May 1872 who went on to greater positions and Mr T.B. Daniel appointed 13th February 1873. Mr C. Willmer was Agent by 1875 but moved on that year. By December 1884 Mr A. Hooper was stationmaster, but he also went to another station with a Mr White taking over on 17th December 1884 ; Mr H. J. Delia was appointed in February 1915. In April 1892 there were plans approved for three cottages to house traffic department and platelayers and these were built on the northern side of the station area, opposite the goods yard. In the summer of 1897 an extension of the loop line was approved by the Directors at a cost of £630. Clearly business was brisk at Itchen Abbas as local people requested further siding accommodation with a cart road on either side. This was initially declined in June 1906 but was granted a year later by the General Manager, by now Sir Charles Owens.

The final part of our journey takes us through some major earthworks, in the chalky downs around Winchester. Some of the deepest cuttings are in this region. The village of Martyr Worthy is just to the south as we go over Chillandham Lane and under Budgitts Farm road and over a footpath. A cart track road appears before we head towards the hump-back bridge which takes the main London to Southampton road (an old roman road) over the line. Just after this the railway passes under the three-arched Stoke

Above: A look at the yard at Itchen Abbas towards the Winchester direction. By now, May 1950, the loop had gone, but the goods yard remained. *Lens of Sutton*

Below: The remote location of Winchester Junction in Edwardian times. The line is seen tightly curving to the south to join the Southampton main line. The families of the signalmen and gangers were housed in the cottages very close to the signalbox. Note the platform by the signalbox which was used to exchange the single line tokens. *MHR Archives*

Railway staff, including the signalman, pose with soldiers during the First World War outside of Winchester Junction signalbox. Various army camps were nearby. *MHR Archives*

Charity to Abbots Worthy road (Lovedon Lane bridge) and over Hookpit Road (Springvale Bridge) on a high embankment. The course of the railway is at about 200 feet above sea level now as the line turns sharply to the south on a curve with a radius of 15 chains, the shortest on the entire line, to reach Winchester Junction in the parish of Headbourne Worthy. This very rural and remote location sees the line join the LSWR's main London to Southampton route. A signalbox is situated in the 'V' formed by the junction. Twenty years after the junction was built, more activity followed in the area with the Didcot, Newbury & Southampton Railway tunnelling its line almost directly under the actual junction points. This railway opened for traffic on 1st May 1885. Just south of this bridge there was a crossover line to get Mid-Hants trains from the 'up' London line to the branch. Works would return to this area in the Second World War when the D,N&S line had a spur built directly onto the main line north of the junction signalbox.

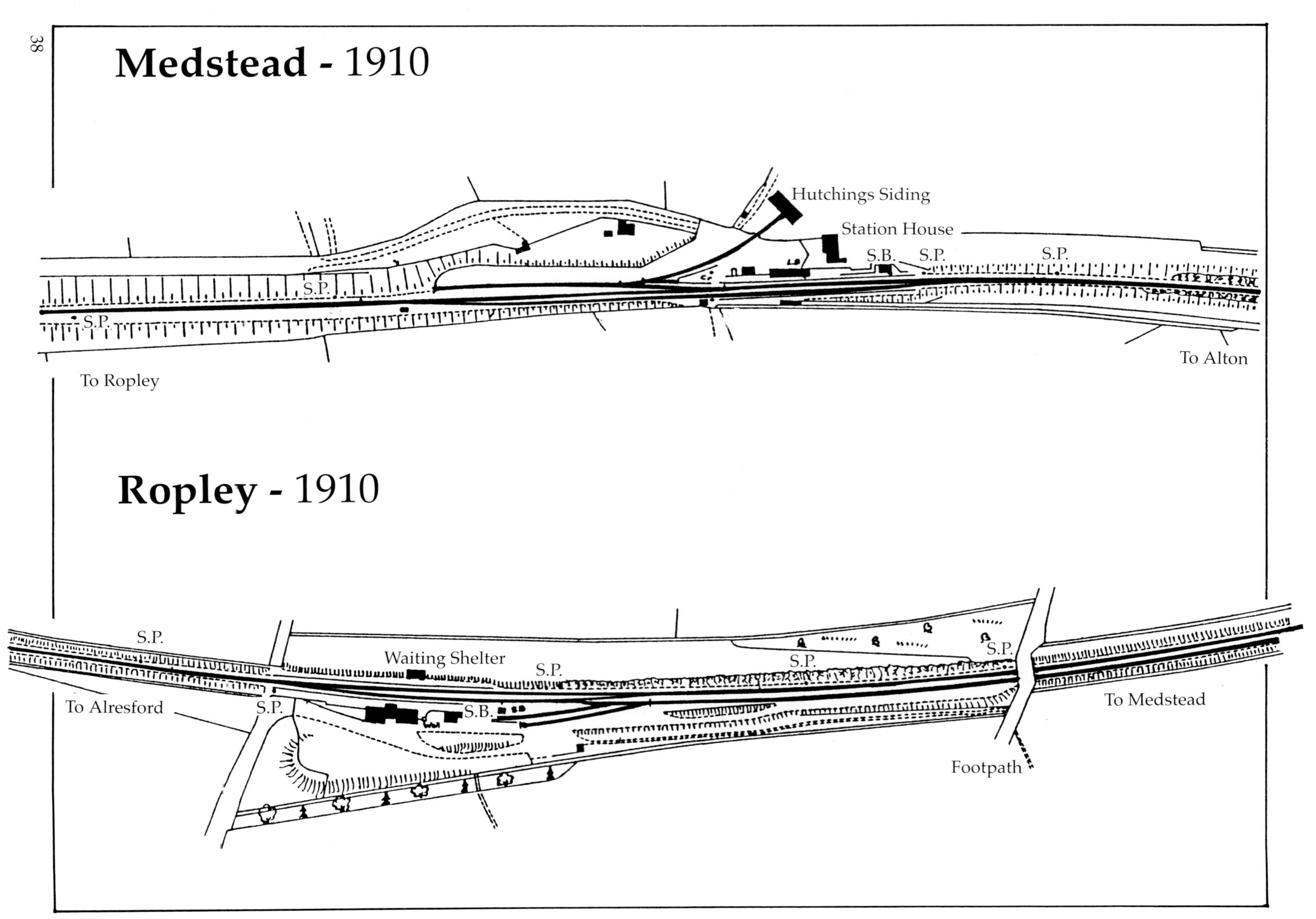

Medstead - 1910
Hutchings Siding
Station House
S.B.
S.P.
S.P.
S.P.
S.P.
To Ropley
To Alton
Ropley - 1910
S.P.
Waiting Shelter
S.P.
S.P.
S.P.
To Alresford
S.P.
S.B.
To Medstead
Footpath

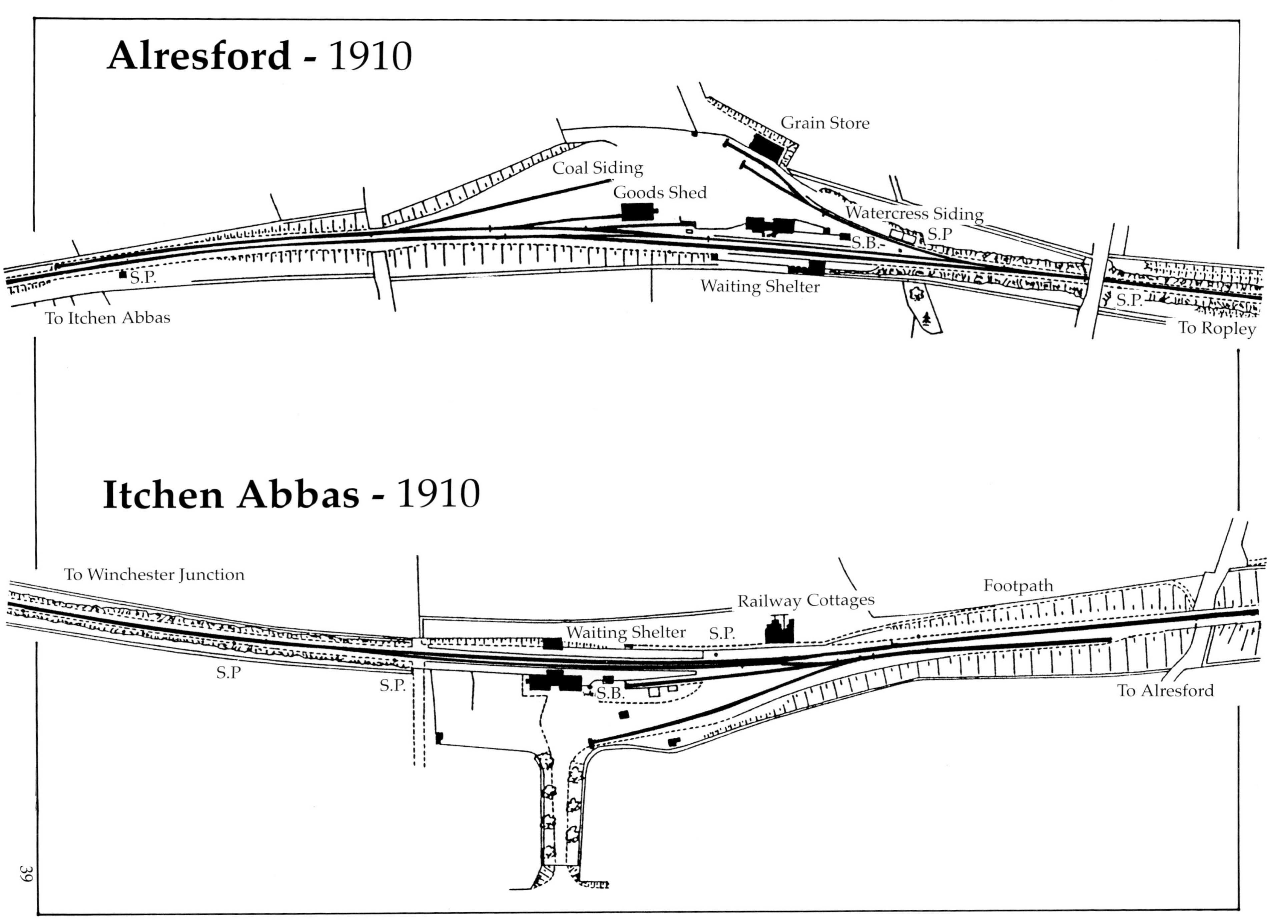
Alresford - 1910
Grain Store
Coal Siding
Goods Shed
Watercress Siding
S.P
S.B.
Waiting Shelter
S.P.
To Itchen Abbas
S.P.
To Ropley
Itchen Abbas - 1910
To Winchester Junction
Footpath
Railway Cottages
Waiting Shelter
S.P.
S.P
S.P.
S.B.
To Alresford

Chapter Three

Development of Train Services

From the very beginning, in 1861, when the line was being developed, it was always the intention of the Alton, Alresford and Winchester Railway Company (from 1865, The Mid-Hants Railway Company) to arrange for its services to be run by the LSWR. The MHR were only promoters and not at all experienced in the running of trains, although negotiations with the LSWR did get to such a pitch in 1876 when the running agreements were due for renewal, that the MHR asked to run their own trains. Director, Benjamin Bateman with shares of £5,000 in the company, offered to put up the finance.

However, returning to 1861, many threats and counter threats were passed between the parties during negotiations for running arrangements on the line. In March 1861 the LSWR board declined to enter into any arrangements following a request by the A,A & WR secretary Mr Porter. Further letters were exchanged and eventually the A,A&WR board were invited to meet with the LSWR directors to discuss the position. The LSWR was obviously concerned that the A,A&WR had running powers in their Bill before parliament for the line over the junctions proposed at Winchester Junction and Alton and therefore onto LSWR tracks. Until this was resolved, it was quite clear the LSWR was not prepared to go any further.

On 4th April 1861 the Traffic Manager, Archibald Scott and the LSWR's solicitor, put to the LSWR board a possible arrangement: "That the board is prepared to recommend an arrangement for working the line and will discuss terms when Parliament have decided on the Bill now pending for the projected Petersfield-Southampton Extension. The board do not object to authorising a subscription to the capital required (for the MHR), but is not to be implied that a pledge is being made for any sum". Furthermore, "that the running powers be withdrawn and satisfactory clauses settled respecting the junctions at Alton and Winchester, the LSWR's petition against the Bill may be withdrawn".

This resolution was put to the A,A&WR directors seven days later when they met the LSWR board in London. At this meeting they (the A,A&WR) gave details of the subscribed capital so far and their 'requirements'.

A working agreement was eventually arranged, although this appears to have been very close to actual opening day, as the *Hampshire Independent* of 8th October 1865 announced the arrangements, six days after opening. The fundamental points were that the MHR were to provide the railway infrastructure at their cost and after satisfactory inspections by the LSWR officers, the latter would arrange all the running of services and provide the necessary staff to do so. In recognition of this the Mid-Hants Railway Company would receive 52 ½% of the receipts.

Opening day on the line must have been a magnificent time for the promoters and local people. After years of planning and concerns over finances they had finally achieved their goal of five years earlier. But would it be successful and would train services make it to London Waterloo and would it be

ON THE OPENING OF THE

Alresford, Alton, and Winchester Railway,

On MONDAY, OCTOBER 2nd, 1865,

By Mess. J. & W. Freemantle, Alresford, Hants.

"Labor omnia vincit."

We have our Railway at last. It has been talked about for many years, 20 years or upwards, and we hope and trust that it will be for the benefit of Alresford and surrounding neighbourhood, and for persons in general. Several poor men lost their lives during the cutting, we lament to state. Masses of earth fell upon them and buried them alive! The Lord God save us from such a dreadful end!!! There are three things says Lord Bacon that make a nation great and prosperous—*Busy Workshops; Ready Money; and an easy transit of goods from place to place!*

financially viable for the shareholders. No doubt these thoughts were left in abeyance on Monday 2nd October 1865 as the villages up and down the line heard the sound of steam and whistles for the first time.

When train services began they were confined to four passenger services each weekday, originating at Guildford in the north and Southampton Terminus in the south. Two of these services in the 'up' direction did go through to Waterloo and one in the 'down' direction originated there. A Sunday service of one train in each direction was inaugurated in December 1865 but was withdrawn the following November.

It's hard to imagine in the 1990s what the scene must have looked like in 1865. The stations certainly looked much as they do now, although we have more buildings surrounding them these days. From the beginning and for many years afterwards, the engines and coaches would have been from the designs of Joseph Beattie. It is amazing to think that one of his 2-4-0 'Falcon' class locomotives or 2-4-0WT engines may have drawn the first train. Certainly he asked the Locomotive Committee on 22nd June 1865 to approve "additional engines to work new lines coming along in 1865; Kensington/Portand branch/Netley/Alton-Winchester/Okehampton". A letter was read out from the locomotive builders, Beyer Peacock, which quoted for six new engines at £2430 each. This was for Beattie's 2-4-0 well tank engine design and the order was for Nos. 203-208. At the same meeting it was said that if another order of six was placed they would be required for £2400 each because of the quantity ordered. This order was duly agreed on 3rd August 1865, for numbers 209-214. It is quite possible these ran the early trains starting from Guildford.

There are no actual reports of specific engines working the line until the period of the early 1900s. But it is clear that before this date and for the remainder of the line's life, virtually every type of locomotive in service at the time must have passed over its tracks.

In September 1864 the LSWR instituted a system of seven 'districts' under District Superintendents with an assisting Inspector. The Alton line came under District No. 6 with a Mr Dyson the Superintendent. His assistant was a Mr Spencer. When Captain Tyler wrote his report on the line before opening, he remarked, "I am informed that this line is to be worked by Telegraph on the same system as the line to Exeter, I consider myself that the Train

Beattie Well Tank No. 200, one of a batch built just before Mr Beattie asked for more of the class to operate the new branch lines then being built. The LSWR had 250 locomotives on its books in 1865. This early view, thought to be in 1885, was taken at Farnham; the engine quite probably visited the Mid-Hants. *J.H. Knight collection*

Staff system, under proper arrangements, is much safer". He went on to say, "only one engine in steam or two coupled together shall be allowed to be between any two stations". The telegraph system was not suitable for more than 'one engine in steam' as the signals were not interlocked and an error by the signalman could result in a serious incident. Interlocking had been invented in France ten years previously but it was not until 1889 that a Railway Act was passed to make the practice law on all lines.

Apart from the signalbox at Alton, there were new ones at Ropley, Alresford and Itchen Abbas and eventually, in 1868, one at Medstead. The completion of the station at Medstead was very much connected with the overall financial state of the Mid-Hants, even one year after opening. On 13th September 1866 the MHR board offered the LSWR £500 to complete the building, but this was deemed inadequate, another £450 being sought to build the Agent's house as well. In any event the MHR then owed the LSWR monies for works they had to do to the line to bring it into order for opening and needless to say the LSWR wanted this before any further works could begin. Eventually, in November 1867, the MHR agreed to pay £700 to the LSWR to complete Medstead and this they did after receiving the amount in March 1868. Mr Strapp, the LSWR's Engineer, was ordered to carry out the works.

All the while this negotiation was taking place there were many requests by the MHR and local people for better services, a situation which continued for some twenty years. It was quite often linked to accusations that the LSWR were deliberately turning traffic away from the line, towards their own main Basingstoke route. But this was always strongly denied.

Meanwhile the journey time from Alton to Winchester was about one hour initially, but this was improved upon when, in August 1866, the LSWR board was told that due to 'alterations' on the line, increased speeds were now possible. This was due to the up-grading of chairs on the sleepers as recommended by the Inspector before opening.

The average receipts for the line seem to work out at about £7000 each for the first three years, giving the MHR approximately £3675 in income. This improved by 1875 with total receipts of £11318 and £5947 going to the MHR. This income is not, however, very considerable taking into account the construction costs and clearly the situation became quite difficult for them. One of the many requests for payment of receipts, on account, was made by Mr Porter, the secretary of the Mid-Hants Railway Company, on 3rd January 1867 when he wrote asking for £2000. This type of letter was sent virtually every six months and clearly shows the company was in some trouble. So much so that from February 1868 there are references to having the traffic receipts paid 'into court'.

One of the main problems was that the line could only get good access to Guildford, until the junction at Pirbright was opened and the line to Farnham Junction installed. This by virtue of the services offered, made the line a branch and not as yet another main link with London. From May 1870 the new line from Woking via Pirbright Junction was available and trains could now go direct from Waterloo to Southampton over the railway. However, from the table of figures below, it did not appear to increase revenue that much, initially at least.

Receipts for 1875

	Local Stations	Through to MHR	Over MHR lines
Passengers	552	2528	4348
Goods	329	1807	1754
Total	881	4335	6102

Other years

	Passengers	Goods
1866	4305	2537
1867	4346	2505
1868	4720	2869
1869	5235	2986
1870	5428	2790
1871	6159	2774
1872	6649	3079
1873	6595	3542
1874	7152	3623

The definite troubles between the two companies culminated in a Parliamentary Commission Hearing in May 1876 to have all the points from both sides aired. The petition at the hearing from the LSWR was that, "works were not completed in time; LSWR had to finish and take off costs from MHR receipts; the MHR had powers only for the 'Alton line' and not for any other course of railway; the MHR had debts of £16,000; LSWR was against MHR having powers to Winchester and Guildford, as possible danger existed, with SER already having powers".

In reply, the MHR director, Mr Henry Hall, owner of banks and breweries in the Alton area said, "LSWR had not worked line well, including goods. Goods to Alton from Southampton often sent via Basingstoke and Woking. Passengers have been diverted from Waterloo to Southampton via Basingstoke, losing revenue". He also said that, "MHR were looking at working the line themselves, by finding directors willing to hire locomotives and he wanted to see powers over LSWR lines. The SER may become supplier of rolling stock".

Farmer Thomas North from Alresford was present and said that, "on Sunday's he had to take his milk to Winchester to catch the train". On examining Mr Charles Collis, the seed merchant from Alresford, the Counsel for the LSWR said, "the MHR was a branch line and could not expect main line services. At 1 in 60 it hardly suited express trains". Mr John Fisher, corn dealer from Ropley commented, "that market was at Winchester, the train arrives two hours before and leaves two hours afterwards".

Benjamin Bateman, original financier and director of MHR from 1875 said, "the MHR had been oppressed by LSWR and he would gladly find money to help MHR run own trains, they were currently badly timed". Counsel said that, "there was no obligation to send trains over the line in the agreement, just to run MHR services".

In summing up, the Committee did not agree to MHR having running powers, but they did suggest the Railway Commission be arbitrators in the future.

It could be said that the MHR was very strapped for cash and this is why they continually pushed the LSWR on the train services issue. Perhaps they were beginning to realise that their dream of a line between Alton and Winchester was not going to make them any richer!

Working agreements raised themselves again in the years 1875/78 and again in 1879. A temporary agreement must have been decided upon in 1875 as the ten year arrangement was clearly due for renewal. In May and June 1878 the question of sharing 'junction' costs loomed, but the MHR were not having it and the LSWR agreed to drop the idea. Instead, on 15th June 1879, Mr Archibald Scott reported to his board that, "new arrangement could be carried out with MHR if LSWR pay them £9500 rent a year from 1st October 1880, to be ultimately converted into purchase of line by paying £237,500, partly in cash and in 4% stock". This arrangement was eventually agreed in August 1880 and on 30th June 1884 the entire assets of the Mid-Hants Railway Company were bought.

Services on the line increased after the LSWR took over completely and there were now six trains each way weekdays and two on Sundays for the first time. There were two references by the Traffic Department regarding the working of trains on the line. Firstly, in 1880, they commented that the Board of Trade, "had required the use of brakevans to be next to engines on every occasion". The second note was by Mr William Adams, the new Locomotive Superintendent, who asked for, "additional brake power on the Alton to Winchester line trains". Obviously the inclines were causing concern; a few years later they would actually cause some destruction.

In the early 1890s, attention was drawn to the method of single line working, which had been in place since 1865. As the Inspector at the time suggested, the Telegraph system was not the favoured option (indeed it was law from August 1889 to provide all lines with fully interlocked signals and points) and in 1892 the General Manager, Sir Charles Scotter, suggested the installation of the Electric Tablet system (this had been invented by Edward Tyer in 1878). The work would cost some £750 to

The 'A12' or 'Jubilee' Class often worked the Meon Valley and Mid-Hants line services in the 1920s. Here No. 638 is about to depart from Alton down the Meon Valley to Fareham on 17th August 1929. This platform, No. 3, was the usual one for the operation of the Meon Valley line. Mr P. Hatch was appointed stationmaster at Alton in April 1923. His salary was £285 per year, of which £38 was taken for the rental of the station house accommodation.

The late H.C Casserley

A 'T9' approaches Ropley in a 1920s setting. According to the engine headcode, the train is en route from Southampton Docks to Waterloo. There is some activity on the 'up' platform with a few passengers waiting and several cart loads of goods for loading onto the train. This is one of the very few views of the line taken in the days of the through services and as such is an important record. Ropley was lit by oil lamps until the 1950s. *MHR Archives*

complete throughout the line and the additional interlocking of points and necessary alterations in signalboxes, took place during 1893 and 1894 with the interlocking costing £1696.

With the start of services to Basingstoke and Fareham, in 1901 and 1903 respectively, Alton must have been a very busy place. This of course heralded the opening of the second line as far as Butts Junction and the signalbox there which was built onto the side of the embankment just west of the iron road bridge.

Train services in the early part of the century saw the spectacle of different engines hauling the direct trains to and from Waterloo. The route was very much a secondary main line, but nonetheless attracted all types of locomotives. The Drummond 'E10' Class was seconded to the line in 1904. These 'double-single' 4-4-0s, were suited to the line as often the coaching stock would comprise just a four bogie set and a six-wheeled van. The 'C8' Class would also be regulars from 1903 and the elegant 'T3' and 'T6' Adams classes were often seen, as were other Adams and Drummond designs, such as the 'L11s'.

When it came to goods workings, the Adams '0395' class were common from the 1880s, as were the 'A12' Class ('Jubilees'). In the early years the line had a goods train from Guildford to Eastleigh (then Bishopstoke) and return, calling at all the stations en route. It would be the First World War when the line saw some of its finest hours, when hundreds of troop trains traversed the route from Aldershot to Southampton. Butts Junction signalman, Frank Hayter recalled that, "I had time to cook my breakfast, but didn't have time to eat it", such was the extent of the traffic over the railway during the war. Three 'X6' Adams locomotives were transferred to Guildford specifically for this work. They were numbers 658, 660 and 665, to be replaced in March 1916 by 'Jubilees' Nos. 638/45/52/54.

The 1920s would see the start of appearances by the celebrated 'T9' Class and the mixed traffic 'H15' 4-6-0s. The continuing six train each way service had 'up' trains worked mostly by Eastleigh shed with 'down' services operated by Guildford or Nine Elms, depending on the departure point. The Maunsell 'U' Class became frequent motive power on these services from August 1928 right up until 1935 when 'D15s', from 1912 vintage and other elderly Drummond designs appeared.

Drummond's 1897 designed 'double-single' experimental locomotive, 'T7' No. 720, the only one built in the class, was to be seen on the weekly 11.10 Fyffes Waterloo to Southampton Docks boat train express and possibly made its last main line appearance on this service on 27th December 1926.

Even Dugald Drummond's 'Bug' made a test run on the line in 1932, after being overhauled following his death in 1912 and a period in store. This was Mr Drummond's private engine and combined coach which he used to inspect his territory. The early 1930s were the years when through workings were to have their final fling, as a great change was to come about in 1937. The late George Woodward, of Eastleigh, was one of the great observers of train services in the area and his notes have been disseminated by Tony Sedgwick and the late Peter Cooper to enable a view to be taken about the line's trains and operations. Here is a glance at some of the observations made by him at his Eastleigh location.

Date	Loco	Duty	Eastleigh Time	Notes
24/ 6/26	144	-	9.50am	Up
2/ 7/26	E287	-	11.45am	Down 2 x 4 sets +van
2/ 7/26	E706	-	1.00pm	Up 2 x 4 sets +van
2/ 7/26	E562	-	7.12pm	Down 3+4 sets + van
13/ 7/26	E685	-	11.48am	Down 3+4 sets n/c
13/ 7/26	E399	-	4.05pm	Up 4 non-corridor
31/ 8/26	E640	-	9.50am	Up
15/ 5/28	E850	39	10.04am	Down
16/ 5/28	E794	39	10.04am	Down
25/ 5/28	E482	39	10.05am	Down
13/ 6/28	E499	39	10.05am	Down
9/ 8/28	A808	226	4.50pm	Down
20/ 7/33	919	283	9.08pm	Down
23/12/33	1625	208	9.55am	Up
12/ 7/34	927	283	9.10pm	Down
21/ 7/34	409	81	11.10am	Down
14/ 3/35	1806	202	12.50pm	Down
22/ 4/35	120	-	4.50pm	Down
24/ 5/35	2327	37	10.05am	Down
24/ 3/36	395	206	4.50pm	Down
24/ 3/36	851	-	7.05pm	Down
26/ 3/36	1413	206	4.50pm	Down
3/ 7/37	464	-	1.00pm	Down
3/ 7/37	1617	-	6.55pm	Down

These notes are just a sample of the hundreds made by Mr Woodward and from them the great variety in motive power can be seen. Many workings would involve a locomotive on its way to or from Eastleigh Works for overhaul, or indeed, on a running-in turn after Works. So a 'Lord Nelson' was witnessed many times, as were 'V' Class 'Schools' locomotives. 'S15s' were rare on the line, but No. 499 did make three visits in the 1928-36 period according to George Woodward's sightings. (In fact No. 499 was recorded three times in the 1950s too.)

Mid-Hants duties - pre 1937

Six trains per day each way, plus summer extras.

First Up -	Winchester 7.18, Alton 7.59. Southampton Terminus to Waterloo. Duty 281 (Elh), H15 usual.
First Down -	Alton 7.59, Winchester 8.42. Woking to Southampton Terminus. Duty 210 later 208 (Gfd). 'U' Class usual from 1928 until swap for 'D15s'. Loco returned on Third Up.
Second Up -	Winchester 8.00, Alton 8.52. Eastleigh to Waterloo. Duty Elh. 'H15s' usual. (First 'down' and second 'up' cross at Alresford)
Second Down -	Alton 8.55, Winchester 9.37. Waterloo to Southampton Terminus. Duty 37 (Nine Elms). Usually 'T14' or other 4-6-0.
Third Up -	Winchester 10.11, Alton 10.54. Romsey to Waterloo. Return working of first down.
Third Down - Mon-Fri	Alton 10.26, Winchester 11.18. Waterloo to Portsmouth. Duty 205 later 208 (Gfd). Engine off at Eastleigh and GWR one takes train on. 'U' Class usual until 1935. Returns on fourth up.
Sat only	Alton 10.04, Winchester 10.48. Waterloo to Southampton Terminus. (Third down Mon-Fri and third up cross at Medstead. On Saturdays at Alresford)
Fourth Up -	Winchester 1.09, Alton 1.50. Southampton Terminus to Waterloo. Return of third down.
Fourth Down -	Alton 3.30, Winchester 4.17. Waterloo to Southampton Terminus. Duty 226, later 206 (Gfd). Loco returns on sixth up.
Fifth Up -	Winchester 4.37, Alton 5.23. Bournemouth to Waterloo. Duty 260 later 258. Drummond 4-6-0 usual. Engine change at Eastleigh.
Fifth Down -	Alton 5.45, Winchester 6.20. Waterloo to Southampton Terminus. Duty 38, later 11 (Nine Elms). 'T14' usual, with other 4-6-0s.
Sixth Up -	Winchester 7.10, Alton 7.58. Southampton Terminus to Waterloo. Return of fourth down.
Sixth Down -	Alton 7.58, Winchester 8.40. Waterloo to Eastleigh. Duty 283(Elh)

Left: The lofty starting signal on the 'up' platform at Alresford in 1953. The shunt-ahead arm, half way down the post (affectionately known as the watercress signal) was used when the daily goods service shunted the yard. The arm allowed freight trains to run by the 'up' starter without a tablet and was thought to be the only one of its type.

Mrs Margaret Blyth recalls the days when she was a child at Perin's grammar school before the First World War. In 1912 Mrs Blyth and her brother would have lunch at the house of Alresford porter, Mr Ursell. He and his wife lived in the first house adjacent to Sun Lane bridge and after quickly eating their meal, with only an hour before school started again, they would rush to Sun Lane bridge to watch the goings on, "my brother had his own toe-hold in the brickwork and I had mine... the attraction was the shunting going on down below in Alresford station. The Drummond engine chuffed under 'our' bridge many times. Shouts of 'double-up the loop line there' were heard from the shunter towards the driver". She added, "the manoeuvring that went on during the shunting fascinated us as if it were a game of chess.....the faraway clanging of the school bell brought us back to reality with only just time enough for us to race through the churchyard, on to Jacklyn's Lane and up Pound Hill".

D.B. Clayton

Below: Alton station staff of 1922. Fifteen members of staff pose on Platform 1 at the station. The stationmaster at the time was Mr Damon and is the third from left in the front row. He lived in the old station building. *MHR Archives*

Above: Another 'T9' approaches Ropley from the Alton end this time in the early 1930s. A very different scene is on view. The 'up' loop has gone, so too has the signalbox. But the topiary is still in good condition. Signalling records about the line have reference to the 'dismantling of the signalbox' on 25th and 26th September 1931. *MHR Archives*

Right: A very clear photograph of the now-named Medstead & Four Marks station. In July 1937 it was declared in the Traffic Committee Minutes that, "as the nameboards are due for renewal at Medstead, it seems an appropriate time to re-name the station". *Lens of Sutton*

The late 1920s and early 1930s were difficult times for Britain, with the deep depression taking hold. It was a time to consolidate and there were cutbacks on the Mid-Hants line. In July 1930 economies were suggested by the Southern Railway. The plans involved the removal of the 'up' loop and signalbox at both Ropley and Itchen Abbas. The saving in costs at Ropley were put at £70 per year in staffing (most probably the signalman's wages). This left the loops at Medstead and at Alresford for the passing of services on the line. The importance of the line to the Southern Railway, who took over from the LSWR on 1st January 1923, was summed up in a report following a Directors' inspection: "These stations (Medstead, Ropley, Alresford and Itchen Abbas) were scheduled for general renovation in 1934, but owing to the unimportant character of the stations and the urgency of work elsewhere, the renovation has been deferred and is scheduled to be carried out in 1936".

The double section of track from Alton to Butts Junction was to see a change in 1935, as the Basingstoke and Alton was closed completely in 1932 (it had been shut in the First World War but re-opened in 1924), it rendered unnecessary the complicated junction at Butts. Although the siding to Treloars Hospital, off the Basingstoke line, was still in use, the junction would be simplified, so that these trains would go directly over the designated Mid-Hants line towards Alton. The Meon Valley then effectively had its own line from Alton past the Butts site. Simply, the

Above left and right: The elegant topiary associated with the station at Ropley was lovingly cared for by the station staff. These two views are from the late 1920s or early 1930s. Later, Mr Walter Woodley was employed at the station and he became the new 'craftsman' involved with this work. *Mrs A. E. Colliver* *Below:* Ropley after the loop line and signalbox had been taken out in 1931. Anthony Bull, who used the line to go to school at Alton in the 1950s, recalls when he lost his cap after leaning out of the window north of Ropley. Such was the dedication of the staff, that Walter Woodley returned his cap the following morning, having walked up the line to retrieve it. *Mike Esau*

The scene at Alton in August 1952 looking towards the west and very similar to the new layout after electrification in 1937. Platform 1, on the right, has an electric unit ready for its next service to Waterloo. The centre line, at Platform 2, is the one used for Mid-Hants trains and non-electrified. Platform 3, is unoccupied, but a 'T9' No. 30338, is stationed in the siding alongside. *D.B. Clayton*

double track had become two single lines. This left the signalbox redundant, after closure on 18th February 1935 and the building was half demolished, leaving a single-storeyed building as a store.

The major change intimated earlier, was that of electrification - not on the Mid-Hants, but from the London end as far as Alton. Electric services began as far as Farnham in January 1937, saving, it was reported, six locomotives and 65 coaches of steam stock.

The 4th July 1937 was to see services commence as far as Alton, via the Aldershot line. On the same day, electric trains were initiated to Portsmouth. There would be two trains per hour to Alton, including Sundays. New parcels and van trains ran to carry the milk and parcel traffic. This all developed from an inspection of the whole line in March 1934. When it was thought that with the coming of electric trains, the Meon Valley and Mid-Hants services would start from Guildford (as the MHR one's did in 1865) and terminate at Gosport and Winchester respectively.

Between then, 1934, and January 1936, plans were drawn up for the scheme which, in the event, saw the branch trains start from Alton. At the same time a new berthing shed and cleaning facilities would be installed at Farnham, as there was no room at Alton. Electric trains would run in and out of Platform 1 at Alton, with the branch trains using the island platform. Alton was a gas lit station and this was retained and improved at a cost of £210. It was also decided to close the link road connecting the two station approach roads, which would save on maintenance costs. Many other alterations were made to the station area, including the provision of reversible working on all three lines through the station and a lengthened Platform 1, at the northern end. After the initial works it was agreed to electrify Platform 3, to save holding trains at Bentley in peak summertime.

All this meant that a new service had to be instigated on the branch line trains. Thus the often fondly recalled years of the 'M7' hauled Push-Pull trains began.

This new era resulted in a complete recasting of timetables and starting points for the now improved service of seven trains each way. Services would now start at Alton in the north and at Eastleigh in the south and although technically still a through route, the railway became very much a branch line.

The weekday timetable for the winter of 1937, using Winchester as the southernmost point, was:-

Winch.	6.50	7.57	10.32	1.32	2.32	4.32	7.22
Alresford	7.09	8.16	10.51	1.51	2.51	4.51	7.41
Alton	7.34	8.42	11.17	2.17	3.17	5.17	8.07
Alton	7.53	8.56	11.56	2.26	3.56	5.56	8.26
Alresford	8.19	9.19	12.19	2.49	4.19	6.19	8.49
Winch.	8.38	9.38	12.39	3.09	4.37	6.37	9.06

Above: The 'M7' era has begun, although this one, No. 242, is a non-Push-Pull fitted version and is pulling a 3-coach set. No. 242 was the very first of the class to be ordered from Nine Elms Works in 1897. In this photograph of an Alton service, taken at Shawford on 31st July 1948, she is in Southern green with Bulleid 'sunshine' lettering. *W. Gilbert*

Below: A true Push-Pull service on the line. No. 128, halts at Alresford on its run from Alton towards Winchester. This locomotive arrived at Eastleigh in early 1948 to work these trains and left three years later. All the air pump apparatus is very evident. *MHR Archives*

Two views of No. 109 which came to work services on the line in 1943. In the photograph above she climbs through the deep cutting under Boyneswood Road bridge just east of Medstead. Below we see her departing from Medstead station with the 2-coach set. These sets were quite brightly coloured, in green or red. *Both, Lens of Sutton*

Services were operated by the now nearly 40-year old 'M7' Class 0-4-4Ts, although some were a little younger, plus a 2-coach set and worked by Eastleigh shed. It was a new operation for this depot, although it did manage the Lymington branch line Push-Pulls in the early 1930s.

The 2-coach Push-Pull sets used initially on the Mid-Hants line were from sets 1-6. These were made up of ex-LSWR coaches, each set comprising a lavatory third brake (with 7 compartments, 68 seats) and a driving lavatory composite brake (2 first class and 4 third class compartments, 10 and 38 seats respectively). These sets were associated with the Mid-Hants right up to another change in train services in 1957. Another type of Push-Pull set appeared in later years; these were sets 31-36, also made up of ex-LSWR coaches. They were formed of a driving lavatory third brake giving a single large guards/luggage compartment rather than the two much smaller compartments on sets 1-6 (4 compartments, 38 seats) and a lavatory composite (2 first class and 6 third class compartments, 12 and 60 seats). A more modern set, No. 662, with part side corridor, was also in use in the 1950s. The sets were painted indiscriminantly in red or green livery and rotated on all Hampshire branch line services.

A look at the view from a Push-Pull coach as it departs from Medstead on 9th August 1954. Note the guard's look-out window. *R.M. Casserley*

The service of seven trains each way remained unaltered for many years, although the non-stop through workings from Bournemouth to Margate and return, which were portions of the Margate to Birkenhead service detached at Guildford, ceased at the start of the Second World War. Slight time changes took place, but the main alteration to the timetable came in 1949 when two further services were added, making nine trains each way. These two trains were actually acknowledging a known fact that two trips over the line prior to 1949 ran unadvertised as they were workmen's trains. One service (from 1942) was a 5.20pm departure from Southampton Terminus which arrived at Alton at 6.46pm. It then returned at 7.30pm terminating at Winchester at 8.10pm. Around the same period a further un-advertised train (this was the only non Push-Pull working at that time and usually a 3-coach set and a 'T1') continued to run for seven years before finally being included in the 1949 timetable. The other service was a duty from Eastleigh, leaving at 4.00pm but not returning from Alton until 6.00pm.

During the 'M7' era the Sunday service remained constant at four trains a day each way. The timetable for 1945 was:-

Winchester	7.59	11.00	3.56	7.21
Alresford	8.18	11.19	4.15	7.39
Alton	8.45	11.44	4.41	8.04
Alton	9.00	12.05	5.00	8.15
Alresford	9.22	12.28	5.22	8.38
Winchester	9.41	12.46	5.39	8.58

This modest service was so timed that two locomotives were required to work it.

Besides the 'M7s', the 'T1s' and sometimes the 'A12' Class 'Jubilees' were used on non Push-Pull workings. In March 1938, for example, the Alton water column was out of action and the services had to be run by the 'Jubilees'.

It is unlikely that the services were timed accurately, but on 18th August 1942 someone did take notes on the 2.26pm from Alton to Winchester. 'M7s' Nos. 48 and 53 were on duty and No. 53 was on that service with a 2-coach set. It touched 63 mph between Medstead and Ropley and 60 mph between Ropley and Alresford. In the Working Timetable for that year the times in each stage were as follows:-

Stage	Down	Up
Alton - Medstead	12 mins	8 mins
Medstead - Ropley	4½ mins	9 mins
Ropley - Alresford	3½ mins	5 mins
Alresford - Itchen Ab.	5 mins	6 mins
Itchen Ab. - Winch.	6 mins	6 mins
	31 mins	34 mins

The scheduled station stopping time was usually one minute, but quite often more at Alresford. So with these added to journey times, the overall journey took

The four original signalboxes on the line were all of the same design. They were fairly standard and were found on the LSWR system in the period of the 1860s. The base was brick-built with a wooden upper storey and slate roof. The timber walls were panelled-in during the early part of the century. This view is of the signalbox at Medstead & Four Marks, which was built after those at Ropley, Alresford and Itchen Abbas. The frame inside had fifteen levers.

MHR Archives

Left: The art of topiary was also a feature of Medstead & Four Marks station, but in a limited way. Here a member of the station's staff 'sits' on the chair carved out of the tree on the 'up' platform. Stationmasters at Medstead included; Mr T. J. Pile, appointed 22nd February 1923; Mr May, appointed 21st April 1927 - resigned 10th February 1929 and Mr E. S. Dolby, appointed 18th April 1929.

Below: A view of the northern end of Medstead's station building. This shows the inlaid post-box and two rows of fire buckets, which were a feature of every station. *MHR Archives*

approximately 41 to 48 minutes. The 'up' services clearly had the longer inclines to negotiate.

The basic operation of these motor trains involved the use of an engine fitted with a compressed air pump; situated on the right-hand side of the smoke-box. This allowed the driver to operate the brakes (although vacuum brakes were still in use on the engine), the air whistle on the driving compartment and regulator, also from his position in the front of the train. The fireman would remain on the locomotive to attend to the fire and water levels in the boiler and react to any message from the driver via the bell system; one ring each time to start or stop the manual operation of the regulator, which was often the usual way of operating this valve. The usual method of operation on the Mid-Hants line would see the engine propel the two coaches to Alton, with the engine leading on the return journey.

During its quick turn-round period the 'M7s' had to take water at Alton's Platform 2. No. 30379 prepares for her return to Eastleigh in 1956. *M. Gunner*

Another long-time observer of train movements in the Hampshire area, the late John Fairman, recalled, "the rather shrill air whistle on the driving car and the 'panting' of the Westinghouse air pump on the locomotive". He also witnessed, "the considerable quantity of parcels dealt with in the large van section of the Push-Pull sets".

At the start of the Push-Pull service, Eastleigh shed found itself with Nos. 45,49,105 and 109 to work the service. These did not stay for long, however, as in early 1939 five other members of the class arrived. These were Nos. 29, 48, 52, 59 and 125 and stayed longer on the duties, two of them, Nos. 29 and 125 remained until the service changed to another form of motive power completely.

During the Second World War two further members of the class came to Eastleigh, No. 53 in mid 1940 and No. 109 in mid 1943. Nos. 52 and 59 left in the same period. A sixth Push-Pull 'M7', No. 128, arrived in early 1948. 1951 saw a complete review of allocations (British Railways had now taken over all Southern Railway locomotive stock) and Eastleigh received Nos. 30379, 30480 and 30481 - Nos. 30048, 30053, 30109 and 30128 left at this time.

The allocation remained fairly constant throughout the 1950s being Nos. 30028, 30029, 30125, 30328, 30379, 30480 and 30481, these were all fitted with Push-Pull equipment. Nos. 30029 and 30125 were the longest serving residents when their term ended in 1957, each completing half a million miles since 1939, an average of 28,000 miles per year.

It is interesting to read more of George Woodward's observations at Eastleigh of Mid-Hants services, this time from the first day of 'M7' workings:-

Date	Loco	Eastleigh Time	Notes
4/ 7/1937	109	10.15am	Second Down train
5 / 7/1937	49	6.35am*	First Up train
5/ 7/1937	109	7.42am	Second Up train
30/ 7/1937	105	6.35am*	First Up train
2/10/1937	60	7.42am	Second Up train
2/ 3/1938	625	10.00am	'A12' Second Down
2/ 3/1938	636	1.00pm	'A12' Third Down
16/ 3/1938	49	6.35am*	First Up train
22/12/1938	642	10.00am	Snow blocked line, first train Up
4/ 1/1939	341	6.50pm	Seventh Up train
9/ 4/1940	29	6.31am*	First Up train
9/ 4/1940	125	7.48am	Second Up train
23/11/1943	125	10.10am	Second Down train
21/ 3/1944	48	6.40am*	First Up train
6/6/1949	30128	3.30pm	Fourth Down train
6/ 6/1949	30029	4.02pm	Sixth Up train
9/ 6/1951	30480	5.45pm*	Eighth Up train
17/ 5/1952	30481	4.55pm	Seventh Up train
8/ 7/1952	41304	7.15pm*	Nineth Up train
27/ 6/1953	30031	5.45pm*	Eighth Up train
14/ 9/1957	30029	3.30pm	Fourth Down train
14/ 9/1957	30125	4.00pm	Sixth Up train
14/ 9/1957	30030	5.05pm	Sixth Down train

* To or from Southampton Terminus.

From these important notes we see the usage of the various allocated 'M7s' during the twenty year period and the occasional 'visitor'. The 'A12', or 'Jubilee' Class, duties were due to the problem with watering facilities at Alton. The 'M7s' would have to refill side tanks before the return journey, whereas the 'Jubilees' had more tender capacity.

Above: A Push-Pull working heads under Borovere bridge in 1956 with an unidentified 'M7'. The two Alton 'up' distant signals are very apparent. *Neil Sprinks*

Below: No book about the line would be complete without the classic photograph taken by the late Edward Griffith at Ropley. His view of 'T1' No. 8 on a non Push-Pull working in 1947, captures the idyllic country atmosphere of the line. The loop has gone though and the 'up' platform all but a memory for those who stood waiting for the London train. *E.C. Griffith*

Above: A clear photograph showing the layout just south of Butts junction in 1956. An 'M7' propels its train, set No. 31, towards Alton. It is about to pass the old line to Basingstoke. This served as a siding to the Treloars hospital until 1967. The line to the left was the remnant of the Meon Valley line which had closed the year before, but still received freight to Farringdon until 13th August 1968. *Neil Sprinks* *Below:* Set No. 34 is propelled out of Ropley on the 11.00am Sunday service from Winchester on 7th July 1957. The 'long' siding at Ropley ran right under Bighton bridge behind the camera. *P. Waylett*

Above: No. 30125, a regular since 1939, halts at Ropley on its duty southwards towards Alresford. The topiary was still a major aspect of the station. *Below:* Long-framed 'M7' No. 30130 arrives at Alresford from Ropley with a set of Maunsell coaches. No. 30130 was a regular from 1954. Non Push-Pull locomotives would have to turn at Alton. *Both, Mike Esau*

Two of the longest serving residents on the line. Numbers 30125 and 30029 had been working services since 1939. The top view of No. 30125 is at the western end of Alresford and shows the end of the goods yard access siding on the left. The view below is taken from the 'down' platform looking towards Ropley and shows No. 30029 propelling its train out of Alresford. Both photographs taken in May 1957. In the peak watercress growing season it was not unusual for a Push-Pull set to have two loaded vans with the produce on the 'down' service which were detached at Eastleigh. This involved a manouvre at Alresford whereby the 'up' train shunted the vans onto the 'down' service. *Dr G. R. Siviour*

Above: The location is Winchester Junction and the Push-Pull service is being propelled on this occasion again by No. 30029. The signalman has just given the driver in the front compartment the single line token. Bill Hurst, who was a fireman on these turns in 1950 recalls, "collecting as many as thirteen of the tokens from the signalman on the first trip to hand back to Alresford's signalbox. *Lens of Sutton*
Right: A non Push-Pull train is ready to start off from Alton in August 1952 behind No. 30032. A service for the Meon Valley is at Platform 3.
D.B. Clayton

The 1950s witnessed changes in some operations. Other locomotives started to appear on the duties. Non Push-Pull trains, the 7.53am, 4.10pm, 7.25pm and at first the 8.35pm from Alton, would see a variety of motive power including Ivatt Class 2 tanks and BR Standard Class 3 2-6-2Ts which from 1952 were seen on the 8.35pm service. Non Push-Pull fitted 'M7s' would also be seen, including Nos. 30030-33, 30127,30130,30133,30242,30243,30324,30356,30375-78,30479,30667,30673 and 30674.

The non Push-Pull trains would use a 3-coach non corridor set numbered in the 1XX series, but other Southern and BR standard corridor sets were also seen, particularly on the 8.35pm from Alton. This

Above: Alresford station staff in May 1946. This is possibly the occasion of the new stationmaster, Mr L.H. Hooks, taking over from Mr Newnham. The staff at the station in June of that year were, W.C. Booth, Porter; J.W. Whitwick, Clerk; Dennis W. Ford, Signalman; Walter E. Norris, Signalman and R.M. Whitwick, Signalwoman. On the occasion of Miss Stella Green, porter at Ropley, leaving to get married, all the staff on the line sent their good wishes. Those at Ropley were, Walter Woodley, Porter, and A.E. Harfield, Porter. From 1927 the stations at Ropley and Itchen Abbas were controlled by the Alresford stationmaster. *Left:* Permanent Way Inspector Turner awards the men on the line at Alresford the prize for the 'winning length' on 'C' class lines in 1952. Names of some in view are, H. Bone, E. Hall, F. Scott, S. Bone, R. Rustell and W. Mensinger.

MHR Archives

service was extended to Swanage on Tuesdays to Fridays in the summer of 1954, with engines changing at Eastleigh. Chris Small, who witnessed these workings, recalls: "I remember the stock was a Bulleid 2-car corridor set (BCK and BSK); the incoming service, the 7.42am from Eastleigh, often conveyed an ex-works vacuum-fitted open wagon on the rear. It would be detached by the Fareham freight engine ('S11' No. 30400 on this occasion) by hauling the whole train into the goods yard, whilst the 'M7' went to the turntable". Chris also recalls that, "during the summer of 1954, the 7.25pm Alton to Eastleigh service was formed on Mondays to Fridays of a 3-car GWR corridor coach set from the Didcot, Newbury line". When the Ivatt Class 2 tanks were quite regular, from 1952, Chris witnessed many times: "When they arrived at Alton up from Eastleigh they were always turned on the Alton turntable, but the timetable did not allow much time for this, as the Push-Pull services came in and went out with watering only. When the Ivatt's passed my house near the line, they were often 'rocketing' by, due to being late!".

During the 1950s the daily freight continued and was worked by Maunsell Q Class locomotives Nos. 30530-32,35,36,42,43 being regulars. Occasionally an Eastleigh '700' Class would appear including Nos. 30306,30316 and 30350, but 'foreigners' from depots such as Feltham could produce Nos. 30339 and 30688. From June 1956 the freight was worked by Guildford depot to avoid the use of the Alton turntable, which was in a rather bad state of repair. At this time the line as far as Farringdon, on the old Meon Valley line, was still open for freight . The locomotives which worked this small service would work the 'down' Mid-Hants goods. Guildford's '700' Class locomotives included Nos. 30308, 30325, 30326, 30350, 30693, 30697, 30698, 30700 and from January 1961, No. 30690. The coal trip from Alton to Treloars siding was always a Guildford turn, at first a Class '700' but from 1953 to 1955 a 'T9' prior to working the 10.20am freight from Alton down to Fareham. On summer Saturdays, when the Fareham freight did not run, a Push-Pull 'M7' could be seen, Nos. 30109 and 30110 were observed.

From June 1956, Guildford shed had the daily duty to run the Mid-Hants line freight. The 'up' goods engine would continue with the 5.02pm from Alton to Guildford and the 'down' goods would leave Alton at 1.35pm for Eastleigh, returning the following day. Class '700' No. 30698 negotiates the section of line approaching Alton with the north-bound return service of four coal trucks and two vans. *Chris Small*

Above: The 'down' freight at Alresford prepares to be shunted in the sidings, access being from the 'up' loop. '700' Class No. 30700 is carrying Guildford's duty No. 110. From 1960 this would be worked up from Eastleigh. *Dr. G.R. Siviour*

Below: A well lit early morning photograph of a '700' Class, No. 30308, on a pick-up goods for stations on the line in 1958. The locomotive is just passing the site of the signalbox at Butts Junction. The top sections of the iron bridge over the main Alton road are visible behind the brakevan and Borovere bridge is in the distance. *Bryan H. Kimber*

Above: One of the very last scheduled Push-Pull workings on 3rd November 1957. For almost exactly twenty years, the 'M7s' had pushed and pulled their coaches along the Mid-Hants line - the following day the diesels came. *Bryan H. Kimber*

Below: Ivatt Class 2 No. 41303 accelerates out of Alresford towards Winchester after shunting the sidings in 1961. The large grain store had been owned by SCATS - Southern Counties Agricultural Trading Society for some time. *Bryan H. Kimber*

3rd November 1957

Farewell to steam-hauled passenger service. Fittingly, 'M7' No. 30029 had the honour of working the final timetabled Push-Pull service on the line. The time is 8.30pm on 3rd November 1957 and a group of passengers and most probably enthusiasts, assemble on Platform 2 at Alton to witness the end of the era. No. 30029 was one of two members of the class to have worked the line since 1939. She had worked over half a million miles during the eighteen year period. After this long duration, she was noted on similar trains in the Tunbridge Wells area in 1963 and at Bournemouth until 1964. No. 30029 was withdrawn in the May of that year. *Bryan H. Kimber*

Driver Brian Aynsley worked these goods services from Guildford shed: "We'd book on at 3.45am to prepare the engine to take it light to Woking. Here we would depart at 5.20am with fish and parcels vans and run to Ash Vale and Aldershot, where the fish vans were detached. The remainder was taken to Farnham where we set back into the 'up' yard and swopped trains with the crew who had worked the 5.00am from Woking. We took this on to Alton where we re-made the train for Medstead and Ropley, sometimes Farringdon or Treloars or the brewery, depending which day it was. Mondays, Wednesdays and Fridays we went up the Mid-Hants and the other days to Farringdon and the two sidings. The Medstead traffic consisted of coal and fertiliser for the agent who occupied the goods shed. There was only coal for Ropley. If we had ten or twelve wagons on and an old '700' we would drop the lever into full gear and sparks would roar out of the chimney, like a house on fire. But we'd usually make it, if only at fifteen miles an hour". He continued, "the tablet for the section from Alton to Medstead had a key on it which unlocked the ground frame at Butts. It could be returned at Alton, which saved going up to Medstead

Above: About to leave the Mid-Hants line, BR Class 4 2-6-4T No. 80035, hauls a reasonably sized freight through Winchester Junction after its trip to Alresford in 1961. One-time fireman on the line, Keith Dawe, said of the line, "when leaving the main line at Winchester Junction, one is immediately aware of the rural aspect, gone is the rush and roar of the main line and in its place there is a slower, more leisurely pace. But when the Mid-Hants climbs, it does so in the shortest possible space". *Bryan H. Kimber*

Left: Ex-LMS 4MT No. 42103 is in charge of the 2.30pm Eastleigh service at Alton on 3rd March 1956. A number of these locomotives and the Class 2 tanks were allocated at this time to SR sheds. *M. Gunner*

to return back again. The 'staff' from Medstead to Alresford also unlocked the siding at Ropley and by putting it into the ground frame it enabled a passenger train to go through whilst we were in the siding".

The '700' class remained synonymous with freight workings on the Mid-Hants line until their withdrawal in 1961/2. From the summer of 1962, Guildford supplied the 'Q1s' for this working, although even Class 'C' 0-6-0s were noted in the form of Nos. 31722/3. But 'Q1' Class Nos. 33001, 33004-6, 9, 12, 14, 15, 18, 19, 19, 22, 25, 32-36 were all observed. Even 'Q' Class Nos. 30541 and 30542 intended for snow plough duties were seen. The 'Q1s' lasted until September 1964 when the Class 33 diesels took over. By this time the only freight working was to Treloars siding and Farringdon. Between June and September 1965, steam returned to this service as the Cromptons were required for ballast workings in connection with the Bournemouth Electrification. All types were employed, but the most unusual sighting was 'West Country' Pacific No. 34008 *Padstow*! Electro-diesels were also employed after 18th April 1966. The last steam locomotive to work the Treloars goods was No. 73115 on 8th March 1967, the last actual working was hauled by E6014 on Tuesday 11th July 1967.

Ideal for diversions between London and the south-west, the Mid-Hants was often used when the main line via Basingstoke was either blocked or had engineering works on it. The line could cope with all types and weights and here's a famous one in the form of 'Lord Nelson' Class No. 30858 *Lord Duncan* on a Sunday in 1956. *Neil Sprinks*

Being an 'alternative' route, a situation which had existed virtually from opening day in 1865, the line enjoyed many special workings, bringing in with them many varied locomotives. Engines from the Central and South Eastern divisions would frequently run 'light' to Eastleigh Works via Redhill, Guildford and Alton for their overhauls. Special trains were also numerous chiefly consisting of boat, troop and empty coaching stock workings. Many were observed by Chris Small and some are tabled below:-

Date	Loco Number	Details
3/1/1957	30861	Troop train
5/1/1957	30698/31631	Troop train
9/1/1957	30350	Light engine
17/1/1957	32451/35012	Light engines
24/1/1957	76028	ECS
25/1/1957	1001	Test run with Hastings unit, 6 cars.
18/3/1957	30310/73050	Troop train
23/3/1957	73111	Troop train
6/6/1957	30547/WD512	LMR 2-8-0 to Works.
21/8/1957	32451	Hauling damaged EMU to Works.
22/8/1957	30910	Light engine
12/9/1957	31625/30027	Light engines
16/9/1957	30777	Light engine

Special Departmental trains

Date	Loco number	Details
15/ 5/1957	73116	Weedkilling train
4/ 9/1957	1101/1102	DEMU test trip
9/ 9/1957	1103/1104	DEMU test trip
14/ 1/1960	M7 class	To examine line after heavy snow.
21/ 4/1960	76013	Weedkilling train
26/11/1960	76060	Track laying between Alton and brewery siding.
27/ 5/1961	30306	Ballast train
7/ 5/1964	1129	Trial DEMU with new 725 bhp engine.
28/ 7/1966	77014	Weedkilling train
14/ 6/1967	73018	Last steam on MHR

These are just a few of the hundreds of special workings noted by Chris Small who has lived by the side of the line since 1950 and has recorded, much as George Woodward did, the movements of trains passing his house. His notes start in 1957 and go through to 4th February 1973 and therefore represent an important log of the last years of the line. Another notable visitor was 'Remembrance' Class No. 32327 which was hauled to Eastleigh Works in January 1956 following its fatal collision in December 1955 at

Left: The Standard class locomotive is dwarfed by the huge Mount Pleasant Road bridge west of Alton as it runs a special diversion over the line. *Chris Small*

Below: A Waterloo to Bournemouth diversion on a Sunday in 1956 is photographed at the Butts Junction. Bulleid 'Merchant Navy' Pacific No. 35019 *French Line CGT* is still in un-rebuilt condition. Three years later it would be rebuilt into an outside valve geared Pacific. *Neil Sprinks*

Woking. Early in 1954 the ex-Southampton Docks Company 0-4-0ST No. 30458 *Ironside* was hauled to Eastleigh from Guildford for scrap. 'Z' Class 0-8-0Ts were also observed in February 1953. Nos. 30950 and 30952 were being transferred to Stewarts Lane. One other peculiar operation observed twice in the early 1950s was the combination of the Saturday 1.15pm Eastleigh to Alton service with a troop train. The Push-Pull 'M7' was coupled ahead of an ex-LMS type (possibly a Class 5 as these were deployed to the SR during the Bulleid locomotive crisis of 1953) with the Push-Pull set on the rear. The train continued to Alton when, on arrival, a '700' Class was provided to work the Push-Pull set back to Eastleigh at 2.30pm.

Chapter Four

Accidents On The Line

Whenever mechanics and speed are involved, it is sadly inevitable that accidents will occur. Many hundreds of incidents, serious and not so serious, are recorded over the years in the records of Britain's railways.

The Mid-Hants line was not immune to accidents and in fact saw its fair share, particularly at the turn of the century. More often than not it was as a result of the so called 'incline' or gradient which reached its summit at Medstead.

Accidents during the construction period are covered in Chapter One, but two of the most significant train accidents occurred during 1900 and both began at Medstead.

The first, on 1st May 1900, involved the 'up' 3.50am goods working from Southampton. On arrival at Medstead station, a portion of the rear of the train broke away and ran backwards the whole distance to Alresford. Signalmen took action quickly to 'turn' the runaway train into a siding at Alresford. Although this brought the vehicles to a stand, they collided with other wagons in the siding, causing quite a shambles. The brakesman, a Mr Charles Campbell, no doubt did all he could to lower the impact speed, but he did receive some injuries.

Two photographs of possibly the most serious accident on the line, on 1st May 1900. Local people in late Victorian dress inspect the mangled wreckage over Jacklyn's Lane bridge. Only slight injury was caused to the brakesman.

MHR Archives

Another view of the accident at Alresford. This photograph is of a wagon which had careered down onto Station Approach Road. The noise of the whole affair must have been heard over all of the town. Two locomotives are in view towards the right of the photograph. One might have the breakdown train attached. *MHR Archives*

This was obviously a most serious incident and of the type forever in the mind of the Board of Trade Inspecting Officer before the opening of the line in 1865. Virtually the same thing happened though eight months later when, on 27th December 1900, after a horsebox had been detached from a 'down' passenger train at Medstead, it ran down the line towards Ropley station. It actually began to overtake the passenger train which had stopped in the loop and collided with the train's last vehicle. Thankfully this time it did not progress towards Alresford.

These two incidents highlighted the lack of precautions at Medstead and, for that matter, at Ropley for runaway vehicles and a year later alterations were put in place at the former location. Major Pringle made an inspection of the works on 8th November 1901. He wrote in his report: "The loop line has been lengthened at Medstead 125 yards at the south-west end. Balance weight catch points inserted on the 'up' loop ascending line to act as a trap for runaways down the 1 in 60 gradient. Being over 200 yards from the signalbox, points are worked from a new ground frame at the south-west end of the 'down' platform. The frame in the signalbox has 15 levers, 3 of which are spare, one is a push-pull lever (this was a lever which could be pushed forwards and backwards to action two signals). All done in consequence of accidents in 1900. The Lamp Room has been moved to the 'up' station yard".

The following two accidents occurred at the other end of the line. Winchester Junction was the location for the first, on 23rd October 1901. An 'up' goods working had stopped at the junction to set down stores for the signalbox. Two wagons were derailed on the crossover, completely blocking the Alton line. A few months later a minor incident occurred when the Lamp Room was destroyed by fire in June 1902. No doubt the inflammable nature of its contents was the cause. The other accident was at Itchen Abbas station and is the only one recorded as happening at this location. The 7.10am goods from Woking to Winchester on 30th October 1902 collided with a horse and cart on the occupational crossing. The horse was injured and the cart quite badly damaged.

There is a reference of a crash occurring to the 11.55 am from Southampton Terminus with a tree between Itchen Abbas and Alresford. This was on 14th December 1908 and so was no doubt due to a period of high winds in the area. A Mr Barnard Curtis was rewarded £2 for attracting the driver's attention and therefore slowing down the train before impact.

Horseboxes seem to feature in many accidents on the line and Alton station saw two incidents with them in 1904 and 1909. The first, in January 1904, saw an engine and horsebox collide with an empty train, blocking the line. But the second, on 3rd February 1909, was more serious in that the 11.20am troop train from Guildford to Southampton ran into a horsebox left on the 'down' line. The horsebox was derailed and the locomotive damaged, but fortunately no injuries. The head porter and signalman were, as the report says, 'dealt' with!

This brings us to another period of rather more serious accidents on the Mid-Hants, including the death of a passenger.

On 10th July 1914, a Mrs Bond fell from a carriage door on the 5.30pm train from Waterloo. Her body was found on the 'up' side of the track at the bottom of an embankment approximately half way between Ropley and Medstead. The report into the incident said that Mr and Mrs Bond were travelling back from London, where she had seen a doctor in connection with her depressed state. An offside door was seen open by a witness.

There were then five accidents during the initial years of the First World War, some again involving the gradient problems at Medstead and Ropley. By 1915 troop train movements were very regular over the line, with many thousands of men being shipped out of Southampton Docks from the important military establishments in the Aldershot area. A return empty troop train on 1st June 1915, with two locomotives deployed, one assisting, came to a halt at Medstead station at 6.45am to detach the assisting locomotive. The train stopped so abruptly that the engines re-bounded causing the coupling between the first and second vehicle of the train to break. All the remaining vehicles ran back towards Ropley but fortunately were stopped by the catch points, inserted in 1901, although the second from last vehicle was derailed.

Just two months later on 6th August 1915, a similar occurrence caused the 10.40am empty troop train from Southampton to run backwards towards Ropley. Again, an assisting locomotive was helping to bring 31 vehicles up from Ropley and they arrived at 12.13pm. They braked so heavily that the train engine coupling with the first van, a South Eastern &

The western end of Alton station on 3rd February 1909. An Adams '0395' Class 0-6-0 ran into a horsebox whilst heading a troop train through the station. The vehicle contained two horses. *MHR Archives*

The station at Ropley seen from the west and across from the 'up' platform. At this point the line is 397 feet above sea level and is on a gradient of 1 in 250. This was the scene of several mishaps during the First World War and in the 1920s, mainly due to the falling gradient from Medstead.

This photograph was taken just before the loop line and signalbox was removed in 1931.

Mrs A. E. Colliver

Chatham Railway vehicle, broke, allowing the train to run backwards. The guard could not apply his brake as he was concussed in the rebound after braking. The 'up' loop points did their work again and stopped the whole lot from careering down to Ropley. One vehicle was derailed. Driver J.R. Brown, of the piloting locomotive, was cautioned for mismanagement of the brake. Lines were blocked until 4.20pm and from that time onwards all assisting locomotives were detached at Alton.

Ropley then saw its share of First World War incidents, all three involving the running by of signals by enginemen. The first involved Driver Burden of the 5.30pm from Waterloo to Southampton, who passed the 'down' home signal while in the 'on' position. He was reduced to shunting duties and guard W.E. Russell cautioned for not keeping a proper look out. Two months later, on 24th February 1916, a troop train with 27 vehicles attached and on its way to Southampton again passed the 'down' home signal. The train was brought to a stand 164 yards beyond. Vacuum brakes were fitted to the first four vehicles only and the guard applied his brake when he noticed his train had gone past the signal. The third case involved the 6.20am horse special from Reading to Swaythling, near Southampton on 8th December 1916. Driver G.T. Turvil was cautioned for passing the 'down' home and guard W. Bright for not noticing it too.

Ropley also witnessed the next reported accident some ten years later, on 19th September 1925. A light engine driven by a Mr Cheesman passed the same 'down' home signal at 8.44am, stopping his engine on the 'up' loop points. A near disaster was avoided because the 7.44am passenger train from Eastleigh was nearing Ropley when it was halted at 8.51am. Through the good actions of Ropley signalman Shoyer, the 'up' loop points were changed in time to avoid being damaged.

The next incident was also at Ropley and occurred on 13th January 1928. It happened at 4.03pm when the 2pm Waterloo to Portsmouth train stopped at the station so that the last vehicle, a horsebox, could be detached. This was to be shunted into No. 1 siding at Ropley, but signalman White elected to uncouple it while the train was in the station and then requested guard Frost to shunt the train backwards to get the horsebox into the siding. This duly happened, but when the train ran forwards again the fourth vehicle derailed on the No. 2 siding points which had been left 'on'. The Portsmouth train had to carry on with just two vehicles at 4.19pm and the 'down' loop was fouled so other services had to use the 'up' loop. Needless to say, all those involved were reprimanded, including Mr Newnham, the stationmaster who was also by now responsible for Ropley as, although he was not on duty, he saw the happenings and did not advise the correct procedure.

Several other de-railings occurred at Alton, although not directly affecting the Mid-Hants line. The first of these was at 8.15pm on 12th April 1929, when the locomotive due to work the 8.18pm to Gosport, down the Meon Valley line, was derailed at the east crossover, blocking the 'up' line. It took until 2.12am the following morning to clear the line and signalman Knight was cautioned for not pulling the points properly. On 31st October 1932 a wagon was derailed, again on a Meon Valley service. The third derailment came on 11th December 1934, when coach No. 4610 came off the points with the 'up' loop to 'up' main line, east of the station. Signalman Hayter and shunter Algar were on duty and cautioned.

The station of Alresford then saw its only major incident since the runaway wagons in 1900. On the 22nd April 1936, at 11am, the locomotive on the 9.03am Waterloo to Portsmouth service derailed on the points at the eastern end of the station. The locomotive was a 'T9', No. 307, and all four driving wheels and tender came off the track. The Eastleigh breakdown train arrived at 12.36, re-railing the 'T9' by 3.10pm. All 'down' trains were halted at Medstead and 'up' trains at Winchester, whilst a broken rail was repaired. A bus service ran in between. The following Board of Trade report stated: "The train had left Ropley at 10.56am. The 8.35am goods from Eastleigh to Alton was in section between Winchester Junction and Alresford (by this time Itchen Abbas had lost its passing loop) so the 'down' and 'up' signals were 'on', as both trains were going to cross at Alresford. Driver Paddon of No. 307 failed to stop his train at the 'down' home signal and No. 7 'down' loop points were set for the loop. The passenger train travelled for 50 yards in a derailed state". The Inspector then went on to say, "Paddon says he could not see the signal until 50 yards from it and that he was travelling at between 15 and 20 mph". Porter/signalman Cornick was reduced to just porter at the inquiry for trying to change points whilst train was across it. Driver Paddon was suspended for two days for not stopping in time.

Before we look at the way the weather affects the operation of trains at times, we will look at the last noted accident, which happened at the last location on the line, Winchester Junction. This happened on 12th June 1938, at 9.46am. The 9.05am 'down' stopping service from Alton ran through the 'down' points on the main Waterloo to Southampton line. This blocked the line and all 'down' services from London via Basingstoke had to use the 'up' line under special arrangements. The due Margate to Bournemouth service, which usually used the Mid-Hants line, was diverted via Havant. Signalman Northover and acting handsignalman Heffer were both cautioned for operating No. 10 point lever instead of No. 11.

Oddly enough, the junction was altered just a year before, in February 1937. To quote Col. H.C. Trench, the Inspecting Officer, he said: "The branch line has a

The scene at the eastern end of Alresford station just after 11am on 22nd April 1936. 'T9' Class No. 307 was derailed after the points were changed during the passage of the locomotive. Just the front bogie wheels remained on the track. The Eastleigh breakdown gang re-railed the locomotive by mid-afternoon. *R.W. Small collection*

The dramatic scene one mile east of Itchen Abbas during the freeze of Christmas 1927. Three Adams tender engines try to push through the drifts to clear the line. In the event it was not until 2nd January 1928 that services resumed. Daniel Bull, a resident of Ropley village in the 1920s, recalls having to spend the Sunday night in the station buildings as he could not get to Ropley village due to the drifts. *MHR Archives*

single junction with the 'down' main line and a facing crossover has been provided between 'up' and 'down' main lines. The signalbox has 'old' frame of 14 working levers and 4 spare. The branch 'down' home (No. 16) is 445 yards from the box. The line is 1 in 110 at this point". He went on to say, "but having regard to the severe limitations of load imposed by gradients on the line and the limited amount of traffic thereon, six passenger and one freight each way, this arrangement is satisfactory". This last comment and his first reference to 'the branch', sum up the feeling the authorities had for the Mid-Hants line. Clearly it was still relatively unimportant to them as a railway, even though its connection was crucial in the First World War for troop trains and would again see this important traffic in the coming Second World War.

The south of England is not known for its severe weather, but over the years there have been times when the 'sunny south' has ground to a halt! The Mid-Hants line does, as we have seen, climb to quite a height at its summit at Medstead, 650 feet in fact, and it can often be a reasonable day in Alresford and a very different story in Medstead.

When snow does arrive in the south, it does seem to affect a large area. This has happened just a few times in the past 70 years, the first major occasion, in 1927, bringing the railways of Hampshire to a grinding halt - the Mid-Hants included. The morning of Christmas Day in 1927 dawned quite mild, but a little wet. The forecast though had bad news for the area; the rain was turning to snow to the north of Hampshire and soon it arrived in the county itself. By 10 o'clock that night it was general all over Southern England. Trains were beginning to have problems, those on the Didcot, Newbury line were stopped, as were the ones on the Basingstoke to Salisbury line. Snowdrifts were developing and Meon Valley line services were having trouble in getting through. All came to a halt on the Mid-Hants Railway and Alresford was cut off completely for the first time in living memory. On Boxing Day 70 men were sent out from Alton towards the west to attempt the clearance of cuttings. The *Hampshire Chronicle* reported, "Alresford stationmaster, Mr Newnham, did his utmost, working in fact like a trojan, to see that the gang carried out their thankless task with as much comfort as possible". A 'down' train did manage to get as far as Alresford that day, but no further and it is reported that two 'up' trains did get away from Alresford, one driver detaching his locomotive to get as far as Alton! The following day, the 27th, a steam plough was sent from the Alton end and got to Alresford and then worked towards Itchen Abbas to free a trapped train. With many drifts up to 35 feet in height, the section between Alresford and Ropley was clear by the 29th, and a shuttle service between Alresford and Alton started. By the Friday, the whole line was cleared, but it was felt unsafe due to the large amounts of snow banked up by the track. Full services did not resume until 2nd January.

As history has recorded, there have been two other major snow falls and periods of extremely cold weather this century. The winters of 1947 and 1962 were both to have an affect on railway workings in the south and the Mid-Hants, with its high embankments would again suffer similar problems to 1927. The line was also blocked in March of 1952, between the 28th and the 30th, a Sunday. It was eventually cleared by the Eastleigh snow plough in time for the early Sunday morning train service.

Chapter Five

Dieselisation and Decline

The year of 1957 saw one of the most dramatic changes in the life of the Mid-Hants line with regard to train services and one which certainly proved to be for the better, for a time anyway. The ubiquitous 'M7' Push-Pull services were by now twenty years old and the locomotives themselves nearing sixty. They had done sterling work on branches in Hampshire and outside the area, but to keep the lines operating and successful, a new source of power had to be found. The Meon Valley line had sadly closed in February 1955, unable to withstand a poor passenger flow. To save the remaining lines the authorities had to come up with a plan.

On 16th July 1957 the Southern Region announced that from 16th September a new diesel train service would be introduced as part of the whole Hampshire branch line scheme; a small piece in the broader British Railways Modernisation Plan of 1955. As is quite often the case when a new service is introduced, it was hoped that it would revitalise the lines in Hampshire within the plan - and it did.

The new services would be for the Portsmouth-Eastleigh-Andover line, the Portsmouth-Southampton-Salisbury and the Southampton-Winchester-Alton lines. Although the other routes received their new Diesel Electric Multiple Units, the Mid-Hants line had to wait a little longer to see the new train service, as only ten out of eighteen of the DEMUs were available by the September. The 4th November 1957 witnessed the first improved service with the new stock and the journey time between Southampton Terminus and Alton was immediately

The newly- built 'Hampshire' DEMUs began their services on 4th November 1957 and started a new and final era on the line. Unit No. 1107 is seen west of Itchen Abbas on 28th March 1965 with the 12.53 Southampton Central (headcode 76) to Alton Sunday train. *M. Mensing*

Above: A 2-car DEMU, No. 1121, is progressing down from Ropley near Bishop's Sutton with an Alton to Southampton Central Sunday service on 28th March 1965. Such was the initial success of these trains that a third car was added to the units from 1959 and the power units increased to 600hp. Despite this additional power they had difficulty in coping with the gradients and had to be reduced again to 2-Car sets. Revised gearing on them allowed the 3-Car sets to run again later on, although in winter they were often reduced to two cars. *M. Mensing*

Below: 3-Car unit No.1123 leaves Alton with an afternoon train for Southampton on 1st May 1966. *John Scrace*

Despite the surge in passenger journeys with dieselisation, this view at Alresford in the early 1960s does not show particularly crowded platforms. 2-car DEMU No. 1105 is on its journey southwards, headcode 16 denoting Southampton Terminus. *Lens of Sutton*

cut to 55 minutes from the 75 minutes for the steam service.

An hourly service was introduced from the start, even on Sundays, and it quickly started to have the desired effect; vastly more passenger journeys were being made. In the first month of Mid-Hants operation, the statistics, which include all new services on the five lines involved, showed an increase of 47.84% in passenger journeys and an increase in revenue of 55.9%.

This was a difficult period in the 1950s, when the country was in the midst of the Suez crisis and petrol rationing had been imposed in December of 1956. This crisis, as in other wars, witnessed troop trains once again on the line, twenty-six running from Aldershot and Bordon to Southampton Docks. The shortage of fuel for motor vehicles no doubt helped the figures, but overall more people wanted to ride the new trains and travel to work or school from, say, Alresford to Alton or Eastleigh.

The communities in and around Alresford and Four Marks were also developing, with new housing in both locations and this too provided new passenger support. There were a few services to Portsmouth for a time and a Sunday service from Fawley between 1959 and 1962 and from 1966 the southern starting point became Southampton Central upon the closing of the Terminus station in the September of that year. The table below details the percentage increases in business from the new service for the thirteen month period to November 1958:-

	Passenger Journeys	**Receipts**
1957		
November	47.84%	55.9%
December	34.27%	33.3%
1958		
January	17.06%	17.31%
February	23.78%	24.64%
March	34.04%	33.3%
April	54.44%	50.8%
May	36.84%	54.86%
June	55.9%	47.3%
July	5.37%	17.72%
August	36.69%	42.58%
September	35.22%	44.61%
October	28.6%	25.7%
November	14.43%	13.49%

In the first six months of the new services, 347,977 passenger journeys had been made on all the lines with the new train services. It can be seen from the

Above: Newly outshopped DEMU No.1121 with full yellow front end, departs from a now forlorn looking Ropley in September 1971 with a south-bound service. This unit and No. 1122 worked most of the Mid-Hants line services until closure. *Below:* Platform 2 at Alton, still the arrival and departure point for Mid-Hants line trains. By now Southampton Terminus had closed and trains used Southampton Central. The initial departure time for most trains from Alton was at 53 minutes past the hour, but this was altered to two minutes past the hour with new timings from May 1968. *Both, John H. Bird*

Above: An unexpected reprieve for the 'M7' service! In June 1958 they had to be brought back to life on the line, due to a shortage of diesel units. No. 30479 looks proud to be back at Alresford with a 3-coach set. *Mike Esau*
Right: From January 1967 omniprinter ticket machines were utilised to issue tickets to passengers on the trains. As the DEMUs were non-corridor carriages, it was sometimes difficult to get all the fares. This photograph at Alresford shows Walter Woodley with his ticket machine. *MHR Archives*

last figure, that for November 1958, that the increase was sustained on top of the first month of operation in 1957.

Interestingly, some teething problems were experienced with the new diesels and in June 1958, 'M7' No. 30479 had to run a substitute service over the line - June saw the largest increase in passenger journeys!

Despite the increase in passenger business, the freight operation was on the decline and declared uneconomic. It was gradually withdrawn from stations on the line between 1960 and 1964, with

Above: Ropley in June 1958. Six months after this photograph was taken, an intermediate token instrument was installed enabling telephone communication between freight train crews at Ropley and Medstead signalbox. This would be in place of the Tyers tablet instrument and allow freight trains to be shunted at Ropley and enable passenger trains to pass. There was a saving of £1100 per annum in wages. *D.B. Clayton*

Below: An overhead view of Alton in 1969. *J. Scrace*

Above: The main station buildings at Alresford in May 1972. A neat row of barrows await anxiously for some business. *Ron Neal*

Centre left: The 'down' side waiting shelter at Alresford. Totem station signs are in evidence as too again are barrows for carting luggage and goods.

Left: The goods shed at Alresford in May 1972. It had not seen business since the withdrawal of goods services in 1964.

Top right: Alresford's 'down' fixed distant signal located to the west of the A31 'turnpike' bridge.

Above: Such was the age and rarity of this 'down' distant signal, that it was requested for preservation by the National Railway Museum - a sign attached to it in 1972 laid claim to it. *All, Ron Neal*

Two views of the Alresford 'up'starter signal. The one on the left was taken in 1951 and shows the lower quadrant starter (No. 14) with the diamond 'shunt ahead' arm half way down the lattice post. This was nicknamed the 'watercress' signal, as it allowed passage of goods engines past the signal to shunt the line to the siding on the left. The photograph on the right was taken in March 1972 and shows the same post, but with a Southern Region upper quadrant arm, the 'watercress'signal had been removed in 1959. The siding into the SCATS store had by now also been removed. *The late E.C. Griffith and Ron Neal*

The signalbox at Alresford on 19th March 1972. The following month the chimney was lowered, even though the line was about to close. Note the large window frame on the right-hand side of the front section. *Ron Neal*

Above: The electric key token machine inside Alresford signalbox. *Above right:* Tyers No. 3 tablet machine. *Below right:* 'Sykes' lock instrument used in connection with the Tyers machine for the Winchester Junction section. *Below:* Alresford's 'up' distant signal. *All, Ron Neal*

Now shorn of its goods yard, Alresford on 3rd April 1966. 'Crompton' diesel-electric Type 3 No. D6506 passes through as a 'Hampshire' unit waits to re-start its journey to Ropley and beyond. *The late D. Fereday-Glenn*

Alresford's goods yard being closed in that year. From 1960 goods workings ran from Woking as far as Ropley three times a week until the goods yard closed in 1963, along with that at Itchen Abbas. It then ran to Medstead twice a week until that yard closed in 1964. The goods from Eastleigh up to Alresford lasted up until 1964. The only remaining freight was then the short working to Treloars siding and to Farringdon.

Exterior view of Alton station buildings in April 1969. *J. Scrace*

Left: A platform view of the main buildings at Medstead & Four Marks. At this time the loop was still in place and the points to the siding on the 'up' side. Medstead lost its twice weekly goods service in May 1964, between 1960 and 1963 it was served three times per week.

Below: The station at Itchen Abbas looking towards the west. The loop line was removed in 1931, some thirty years before this photograph, but now the sidings have been taken up too. It's hard to believe that a young Samuel Fay first started his railway career here in 1872 as a junior clerk. He went on to become Superintendent of the Line on the LSWR then General Manager of the Great Central Railway and became a knight of the realm.

MHR Archives

Six years after the line had its new service of diesel trains a great shock was to ripple over the whole British Railways network. In 1963 Dr Beeching was announced as the new chairman of BR and with him came the infamous Plan, more commonly known as the Beeching Axe. His proposals were for widespread closure of branch and secondary lines throughout the country. His endeavours to close the line are dealt with in Chapter Seven.

Even though the diesel units increased business dramatically, especially in the early years of operation, like many forms of transport in the early

Above: A view looking west from Medstead & Four Marks station in 1956. The goods yard on the 'up' side is evident and the long loop line in the middle distance as instigated in 1901 after the series of runaway vehicles. The original loop points were located at the foot crossing.

V.B. Orchard, courtesy R. Neal

Left: The remains of 'Hutchings' siding at Medstead & Four Marks station in June 1972.

Below: A sign to direct foot passengers to the station. This was sited close to Boyneswood Road bridge at which point there was a footpath to the station. *Both, Ron Neal*

Above: The station 'totem' signs at Ropley and Itchen Abbas as photographed in 1972. Even though the stations were now unstaffed, the clock at Itchen Abbas, at least, continued to work.

Left: The southern elevation of Ropley station buildings in 1972. As with other stations on the line, it was rendered to protect it from the prevailing weather. The porch over the house entrance was also built to protect the doorway from the weather. In an article by the late Edward Griffith in the *Hampshire Chronicle* for 29th December 1972, it was stated that when the well mechanism at Ropley was beyond repair, water was obtained from a locomotive tender parked near the station until a mains supply was obtained in 1955. *Both, Ron Neal*

Right: A view of Itchen Abbas station site in July 1972. These railway cottages were located to the north of the station area and were sanctioned for erection by the LSWR in April 1892. Two were for the Traffic Department and one for a Platelayer. Note the 'trespassers' sign. *Ron Neal*

Above: Ropley on 3rd April 1966. The station looks quite orderly considering it was going to lose its staff in nine months time. It is interesting to compare with earlier photographs the formation and growth of the topiary. The station was converted from oil lighting to electric in 1955 and provided with concrete lamp posts. *J. Scrace* *Below:* Medstead & Four Marks is devoid of its loop line, almost exactly one hundred years since it was opened. The signalbox was removed in 1969.

Above: The station at Alresford during the early 1960s. New Southern Region upper quadrant signalling has been installed, but the future is not bright. *Lens of Sutton*

Below: 3-Car DEMU No. 1107 arrives at a deserted Ropley station on 25th June 1972. *Chris Small*

Above: The 'up' and 'down' service trains cross at the only stage on the line where a loop exists - Alresford. DEMU's Nos. 1101 and 1121 have varying front -end displays. The inverted black triangle on set No. 1101 was to indicate to platform staff which end the brake van was in. The station remained gas lit throughout its life.

MHR Archives

Right: Signalman Dennis Ford passes the single line token to the driver of a 'down' train in the 1970s. *The late E.C. Griffith*

An interior view of an 1860s signalbox in the 1970s. Dennis Ford worked at Alresford station for over thirty years and worked alongside his colleague, Walter Norris. Mr Norris was employed on the line for thirty-five years and was the last one on duty at Alresford when the line closed in 1973. He has recounted stories from the Second World War years, when the box had to be kept open at night for the many troop movements. Alresford station was also hectic with Canadian and United States army men arriving for transfer to their base at Northington Grange. He also recalled the time when, just before D-Day, a 'potato special' arrived at Alresford from East Anglia. They were unloaded and stored in a field nearby, where they stayed for a very long time. They were left decomposing for over a year before they were dug in! Another memory was, "when freight services were so popular, the week before the yard's closure, an embargo had to be put on any more goods coming in". *The late E.C. Griffith*

1960s, the train was giving way more and more to the motor car.

The Mid-Hants line saw a general decline at this time but continued a good trade in diversions as we will see in the next chapter. Itchen Abbas lost its staff from 6th September 1965 when conductor/guards were introduced on the DEMU services. From 2nd January 1967 Ropley became unstaffed and three weeks later those at Medstead & Four Marks left their positions along with the closure of the signalbox and loop line. This left Alresford the only station with staff on most weekdays and at which trains could cross each other in the loop line. Gradually the stations became quite ghostly and as in the case of the booking areas at Itchen Abbas, were boarded up.

The line, which seemed to have so much life in it a few years earlier, was beginning to die.

Right: The transport by rail of watercress continued in a small way until closure, but by now most growers had arranged their own road transport to far off markets. *The late E.C. Griffith* *Below:* After the station at Itchen Abbas became un-staffed, the buildings were boarded up to try and prevent vandalism. The ultimate vandalism would come in the late 1970s as the station was demolished by contractors to make way for new housing. *MHR Archives*

The Booking Office at Alresford station in March 1972. In March 1920 plans were announced for a £109-improvement to Alresford's Booking Office. Prior to that it was a small affair close to the main doorway of the station and had a curved outer wall with booking window. *Ron Neal*

Chapter Six

A Diversionary Route

Despite being a secondary route and somewhat forgotten by the authorities, the line has, over the years, had a crucial role to play in the area. We have already seen how important it was in the various conflicts of the twentieth century, with hundreds of troop trains traversing its course. Because it was an alternative railway link from London to Southampton, albeit a slower one as history has told us, the line was used extensively for diversions when the main route via Basingstoke was blocked or in need of engineering work.

Between 1965 and 1967, the main line was having major investment in third rail electrification and this made it necessary for the line to be closed at times for the work to be carried out. It was not the first time the Mid-Hants line had come to the rescue and there followed over the two years many diversions of main line train services, including the celebrated 'Bournemouth Belle' Pullman service. In the latter period of this new trade for the line, in January 1967, Medstead & Four Marks station lost its signalbox and loop line and the diversions had to be skillfully timed to link in with the hourly local diesel service. This left the passing loop at Alresford only in use.

The following pages are a record of these diversions from the 1950s to the end of steam operation on the SR in 1967. Chris Small's observations are also noted in a brief form, as again they stand as a useful record of the types of trains and locomotives travelling over the line during this interesting period.

A Sunday diversion in 1956 with un-rebuilt 'West Country' Pacific No. 34018 *Axminster*. The train is probably a Southampton Docks special and has just passed the old Basingstoke line junction at the Butts. On this particular day the main line had engineering works on it. *Neil Sprinks*

Above: A view at the northern end of Alton station and a diverted Bournemouth to Waterloo service leaves Platform 2 in January 1961. BR Class 5 No. 73082 *Camelot* is the motive power and the old station building can just be seen behind the tender. *Below:* Another Bournemouth to Waterloo express runs into Alton from Medstead & Four Marks. 'Merchant Navy' Class No. 35008 *Orient Line* hauls a variety of Bulleid and Maunsell stock in this January 1961 view. *Both, Bryan H. Kimber*

Left: Because of the inclines, particularly on the section up to Medstead station, it was often prudent to attach an assisting locomotive. This would be detached at Alresford and run light back to Alton for its next turn. In 1956 a 'Battle of Britain' hauled express from Waterloo is assisted by a '700' Class, No. 30700, over the section around Butts Junction. *Neil Sprinks*

Below: After attaching 'U' Class No. 31628 at Alton, the most famous regular train to run out of Waterloo, 'The Bournemouth Belle', departs with a re-built light Pacific in January 1961.

Bryan H. Kimber

Above: The flurry of diversions in 1961 was caused by an earth slip at Hook on the main line. From 5th January to the 23rd 128 train and light engine movements were recorded over the Mid-Hants line, including this one hauled by 'West Country' Pacific No. 34037 *Clovelly* on 8th January 1961 at Alresford. The service is the 13.30 Waterloo to Bournemouth. *Below:* On the same day, Ropley witnesses the passing by of 'The Bournemouth Belle'. Perhaps the original promoters of the line in the 1860s had realised their dream of through services from London after all. *Both, the late D. Fereday-Glenn*

Above: With electrification work continuing on the main line, No. 34019 *Bideford* has No. 80151 attached for assistance on the 0954 Weymouth to Waterloo on 15th May 1966. The train is seen passing through Itchen Abbas. *J. Scrace* *Below:* On the same day, the 0855 Bournemouth to Waterloo has a stranger to the region at its head; ex-LMS Class '5' No. 45493 is seen passing the Butts on its way to Alton. *Chris Small*

Above: By 1966 'The Bournemouth Belle' was scheduled for diesel haulage. Here D1686 operates the 'down' service on 1st May 1966 out of Alton. *Below:* The 0933 Waterloo to Bournemouth is double-headed through Medstead & Four Marks behind No. 34023 *Blackmore Vale* and pilot engine D6577 on 18th September 1966. During this weekend of diversions 48 were recorded over the two days.

Both, J. Scrace

Table of Diversions over Mid-Hants Line from 1961 to 1967

Date	Time at Butts	Loco	Details
5/1/1961	1100	30862	Up Ocean Liner Express
5/1/1961	1130	34053	Bmth West to Waterloo
5/1/1961	1200	30865	Down Soton Docks
5/1/1961	1305	30859	Up Ocean Liner Express
5/1/1961	1510	31628	Light Engine from Alresford
6/1/1961	1115	35027	Bmth West to Waterloo
8/1/1961	1350	35018/ 31628	Bournemouth Belle
8/1/1961	1450	34037	Waterloo to Bmth West
8/1/1961	1510	31628	Light Engine from Alresford
9/1/1961	1120	35008	Bmth West to Waterloo
9/1/1961	1200	30698	Light engine to Alresford
9/1/1961	1240	73118/ 30698	Weymouth to Waterloo
9/1/1961	1610	80144/ 34040	Weymouth to Waterloo
9/1/1961	1720	80144	Light engine to Alresford
11/1/1961	0955	31636/ 34102	Waterloo to Bmth West
11/1/1961	1315	31636	Light engine to Alresford
11/1/1961	1610	31636/ 35020	Weymouth to Waterloo
17/1/1961	1610	76015/ 35005	Weymouth to Waterloo
17/1/1961	0930	76006/ 35029	Bmth West to Waterloo
23/1/1961	0930	76026/ 35012	Bmth West to Waterloo
10/1/1965	0430	73082	Waterloo to Soton Terminus
14/1/1965	0035	80065/ 34023	Theatre train Waterloo to Bmth Central
16/1/1965	2330	D6549	Vans Clapham to Eastleigh
24/1/1965	0225	35028	Weymouth to Waterloo
20/4/1965	1630	33006	Light engine Elgh to Gdf
29/5/1965	2330	D6528	Vans Clapham to Eastleigh
1/ 8/1965	0410	73114	Waterloo to Poole took 24 mins from Alton- Medstead
8/ 8/1965	0430	35017	Waterloo to Soton Terminus
19/9/1965	0405	73083	Waterloo to Poole, took 54 minutes Alton-Medstead
3/10/1965	0430	D818	Waterloo to Soton Terminus
3/10/1965	0800	D818	Eastleigh to Waterloo
21/10/1965	1910	1102	DEMU returning from Longmoor after filming 'St. Trinian's Train Robbery'
6/11/1965	0005	34023	Waterloo to Weymouth. Stuck on bank assisted by engine off 2335 from Waterloo then at Alton
6/ 3/1966	1030	35028	Waterloo to Bath S&D tour
4/ 9/1966	0955	D6512	TC's 404/5/8 first seen
11/6/1967	1100	D6501/ 34093	Last steam hauled train on line - Waterloo to Bmth
4/ 2/1973	2250	D6511	4TC426/06 LAST TRAIN ON LINE.

Although local services were not normally affected, on Sunday 8th May 1966 they were replaced by a bus service. After Medstead loop was closed in January 1967 some local trains were halted at either Alresford or Winchester to allow extra pathways for diversions and buses worked in between.

'West Country' Class No. 34002 *Salisbury* hurries through Itchen Abbas on 1st May 1966. *John H. Bird*

Chapter Seven

A Fight for Survival

Dr Beeching had declared a wish to close the Mid-Hants line in his plans of 1963, but the hundreds of diversions over the line in the 1960s would breathe some life into an otherwise declining railway route. Another spin-off of closure threats was the running of many special trains.

The mid-1960s was also a time when BR were running down the use of steam on the Southern Region, the electrification of the main line from Waterloo to Bournemouth being an example of the new era of traction. Because of the dual threats of line closures and steam locomotive withdrawals, many excursions were run all over the region and several passed over the Mid-Hants line.

In September 1960 the Locomotive Club of Great Britain's special 'South Western Limited' railtour went down the line behind 'L' Class 4-4-0 No. 31768. A few weeks later, on 15th October 1960, an 'M7' working returned to the area. No. 30028, fitted with Push-Pull equipment, worked a set of two carriages along to the siding at Treloars and then down the remains of the Meon Valley line to Farringdon.

Other specials in the south would commemorate the passing of a particular type of locomotive. In 1966 the one and only 'S15' Class 4-6-0 in service, No. 30837, a Maunsell variety, ran two trips to Eastleigh Works over the line from Waterloo. The first was so successful that another was run the following weekend. On 9th January 1966 No. 30837 worked the first of these specials through Alton at 12.05pm having departed from Waterloo at 9.15am. The second run, the following Sunday 16th January 1966, saw the region covered in snow, so the spectacle of the 'S15' and this time a 'U' Class No. 31639 attached, was such

'L' Class 4-4-0 No. 31768 leaves Alton station for its trip over 'the Alps' with its LCGB special on 14th September 1960.
Bryan H. Kimber

Above: 'M7' No. 30028, which had been a latter-day performer on Push-Pull trains up to 1957, is greeted at Platform 2 in Alton's station by Station Foreman Len Hillyer after arriving back from working the 2-coach special down to the Treloars siding. Afterwards it proceeded down to Farringdon on the remains of the Meon Valley line.

Bryan H. Kimber

Right: Taken a little earlier on the 15th October 1960, the 'M7' is propelling its train into the Treloars siding. A member of the crew has just operated the ground frame controlling the siding.

The late E.C. Griffith

that it drew more photographers to the line than the previous week!

Three more tours were to be seen on the line during 1966. On 27th February 'Merchant Navy' Pacific No. 35028 *Clan Line* worked the 'Dorset Belle' special to Weymouth from Waterloo, running through Alton at 10.05am. The locomotive returned a week later to haul the 'Somerset & Dorset Line' closure railtour of 6th March. Driver of No. 35028, George Porter, remembers, "the load was 335 tons, ten coaches, quite enough for 'the Alps'. We stopped at Alton for water and then speed rose to the mid-forties quite soon, reaching Medstead summit at 36 mph. Competently assisted by my fireman, Les Golding, the engine went up the bank like a donkey chasing a carrot, so much so that Inspector Jupp suggested I pull back on the regulator in case we ran by the home

Left: Maunsell 'S15' No. 30837 pulls into Alresford with the first of the 'S15' Commemorative Railtours on 9th January 1966. The fireman is ready to hand the single-line token to the signalman. *John H. Bird*

Below: The following week's run of the LCGB tour saw the Mid-Hants line covered in snow. For assistance up the incline 'U' Class No. 31639 was attached. *Mike Esau*

Right: As part of its Wilts and Hants railtour on 3rd April 1966, the LCGB route took in the Mid-Hants line on the return leg from Salisbury and Southampton. Nos. 31639 and 33006 leave the cutting at Alresford on their way to Alton and eventually Waterloo.This train was the last 'Q1' working. 'Q1', No. 33006, had been withdrawn in the January but kept on to work this tour and another a few weeks earlier. *J.S.Everitt*

Below: Here's one that ran earlier - in 1964 in fact. On 24th September the line was visited by the last steam locomotive built by BR, No. 92220 *Evening Star.* Sporting its headboard 'Farewell to Steam Tour', the locomotive and train is seen approaching Alresford from the Ropley direction just after crossing the A31 bridge. *John H. Bird*

signal. We paused at Alresford to pass over the tablet and then went on to Christchurch for a crew change".

Then, on 3rd April, the 'Wilts and Hants Railtour' passed up the line from Salisbury at 6.10pm through Alton with Nos. 31639 and 33006 in charge. These were all run on days when a good number of diversions were also routed over the line.

All these trains were using the line as a route to another destination. Soon the line would see its own trains marking the end of the railway between Alton and Winchester.

It was always hoped that the strategic value of the route would make BR retain the line. But alas no, once the electrification to Bournemouth was complete, it was considered unnecessary to keep the Mid-Hants line operable.

Closure notices were issued for the line's services and stations in 1967: "The section of line from which it is proposed to withdraw all passenger services extends for a distance of 16 miles 76 chains from Alton where it is connected to the electrified London line, to a junction 2 miles 7 chains from Winchester station on the main Waterloo-Weymouth line. The line is single track throughout with a passing loop at Alresford".

BR clearly had a problem as these notices sparked off a huge campaign against closure and objectors in the area began to put forward their views. Local people up and down the line, local councils included, all began to fight the threat. John Taylor, then Deputy Clerk to Winchester Rural District Council, was put in charge to lead the campaign on behalf of the councils and there followed many meetings and items in the press. One thousand objectors to the closure were recorded and this required by law the holding of a

hearing by the region's TUCC (the South Eastern Area Transport Users Consultative Committe).

A meeting was duly called for 18th April 1968 at Perin's school in Alresford and started to hear the references to the hardship that might be caused if the line closed. Every objector received a letter from the TUCC in the January of 1968: "Enclosed for your information is a copy of memorandum prepared by BR giving detailed particulars of this proposal. In accordance with Section 56(9) of the Transport Act 1962, the duty of the TUCC is to report to the Minister of Transport on the hardship, if any, which they consider will be caused by the withdrawal of this passenger train service. They will also make proposals for alleviating that hardship. They are not empowered to deal with any other questions, such as BR's reasons for proposing to withdraw the service". In closing the letter said, "after the Committee have made their report the decision on whether the service should or should not be withdrawn will rest with the Minister."

Left: There appears to be no hurry to begin the 'down' service from Alton to Eastleigh in this 1973 view. The signal is ready for departure, but would soon be put at danger for good. *The late E.C. Griffith*

Below: The junction layout in 1960 at Winchester Junction, looking northwards towards Basingstoke. The line to the left is the Didcot, Newbury line and the Mid-Hants curves away to the right. *Edwin Wilmshurst*

A further letter was sent out on 8th February 1968 informing objectors of the proposed meeting on Thursday 18th April. About a week prior to this meeting, the TUCC provided a summary document listing some objectors' comments and replies from British Railways. The main arguments, as can be imagined, revolved around the journey times to or from work, school or for shopping trips. BR for their part cited the alternative bus times from the Aldershot & District Traction Co., who operated service No. 14 down the route similar to that taken by rail. Eighteen bus services were to be operated each way on weekdays with an additional ten to or from Alresford and Winchester each way (two of which would start at Ropley). Buses would take on average a further twenty minutes to complete the journey between Southampton and Alton and apart from Alton, they picked up passengers along the A31 road rather than at station locations. The departures from Alton were timed to coincide with the train service to Alton from London, which arrived at 49 minutes past the hour for most of the day. Other bus company services were also cited; the Wilts & Dorset Motor Services route from Alton to Medstead village; Warrens Transport Ltd., (Altonian Coaches) operated a service to Medstead on Tuesdays, Fridays and Saturdays and Liss & District Omnibus Co. who provided a service on Tuesdays from Alton to Four Marks and Ropley.

British Railways also provided comparison fare structures, those by rail and by bus. A second class day return fare by train from Alresford to Alton, for instance, was 3s 9d compared to 4s 2d by bus. The journey by rail from Alton to Winchester and return was 6s 3d and by bus 6s. Monthly season tickets were generally cheaper on the bus services. For the longer journey, that say, from Alresford to London and return, the daily cheap day return fare was 17s 6d by rail and would be 18s 8d by bus and rail (bus to Alton then train to Waterloo). For those wishing to travel regularly, the proposed new quarterly season ticket for the bus/train journey was to be £42 1s 6d compared to £35 13s 0d and it took two hours forty nine minutes instead of one hour forty three minutes!

It would be these longer journeys and those for school and college students to Winchester, Eastleigh and Southampton that gave the inquiry its most important findings coupled with local concerns about the ability of the Aldershot & District Traction Co. to fulfill its timetable and cope with peak-time services.

The TUCC also produced some statistics supplied by British Railways concerning the general finances of the line. (These were later to be contested.) It declared that the annual passenger earnings were £50,000 and that expenses were £70,900.

Estimated renewals expenses for the five year period from 1968 to 1972 were; 1968 £28,930; 1969 nil; 1970/72 £12,000. BR also provided several passenger loadings tables for some days in 1967:-

Week commencing 21st August 1967

Daily average passenger loadings

Down Services

Service	0708		0752		0952		1652		1852		2052	
	J	A	J	A	J	A	J	A	J	A	J	A
Alton	7		14		19		23		18		5	
Medstead	5		7	1	3			8	1	8		1
Ropley	1		5		3		1	2	1			
Alresford	7	2	6	3	6	1	3	4	2	4		1
Itchen Ab.	2				2		1					
Winchester		10		20		9		4		4		1
R.O.B.		10		8		23		10		6		2

Week commencing 13th November 1967

Service	0708		0752		0952		1652		1852		2052	
	J	A	J	A	J	A	J	A	J	A	J	A
Alton	9		26		11		29		20		4	
Medstead	5	1	30		4			2	1	1		1
Ropley	5		6		1	1		2	1	1		1
Alresford	10	1	30	6	3	3	9	9	2	6		1
Itchen Ab.	1		6									
Winchester		12		56		4		4		4		
R.O.B.		16		36		11		14		4		

Up Services

Week commencing 21st August 1967

Service	0714		0817		1017		1617		1717		1817	
A.O.B.			11		8		9		20		21	
	J	A	J	A	J	A	J	A	J	A	J	A
Winchester	7		7		4		13		30		15	
Itchen Ab.		1				1						2
Alresford	7	1	4	10	2	2	3	8	4	13		9
Ropley	2		1		1	1		2	1	6		2
Medstead	17	1	4	1	4		1	6		6	2	5
Alton		30		16		15		10		30		20

Week commencing 13th November 1967

Service	0714		0817		1017		1617		1717		1817	
A.O.B.			10		3		36		22		14	
Winchester	6		9		2		25		29		11	
Itchen Ab.			1							1		
Alresford	9		35	12	1	2	48	13	5	19		6
Medstead	10	1	19		3		2	65	1	13	2	3
Alton		27		64		7		22		20		16

J - joining
A- alighting
A.O.B. - Already On Board
R.O.B. - Remaining On Board

These figures are from the peak morning and evening trains. Alresford and Medstead seem to have most of the business of all the four stations on the line, with traffic quite hectic at Medstead during the school term in November compared to the August holiday period.

The TUCC's overall responsibility was constrained to the, "hardship they consider will be caused by the closure"; they may also, "make proposals for alleviating that hardship". There was sufficient evidence heard at the two-day inquiry for the TUCC to recommend that the Minister defer the closure notice. Clearly the many arguments put forward by the local objectors had the desired affect, but it was to be only a temporary halt in the closure proceedings.

It was clear that BR still wanted to close the line and to some extent the poor passenger journeys at times other than peak periods (the service was for 17 trains each way Mondays to Fridays and 14 on Sundays) were witness to the declining business. The stations at Ropley and Itchen Abbas hardly provided any traffic at all and with the loss of all goods services some four years previously, it didn't look good at all.

Pictured from the window of a 'down' DEMU service from Alton, the single line token is collected from the driver by signalman John Brown at Winchester Junction on 23rd July 1972. John Brown was one of the last signalmen to operate the signalbox at Medstead which closed in 1967.

Ron Neal

During the run-up to the inquiry, on Sunday 7th January 1968, two trains were diverted again over the line, reiterating the local feeling that the line was important for this eventuality as well as providing the local train service. Each of the diversions was formed of eight coaches, non electric stock, and stopped at all stations on the line as a replacement for the DEMU local service. Another interesting development appeared in 1970. On the 24th June of that year, Class 33 No. 6531 hauled a 4 VEP EMU, No. 7747, along the line as a 'shoe clearance test run'. This was to ascertain the possibility of loco-hauling electric stock down the line in the event of problems on the main line. But in view of the closure proceedings it was felt insensitive to run further diversions! March 1971 saw the last diversions in the form of the newspaper trains to Southampton and Fareham.

With the electrification of the main line to Bournemouth it was considered in some circles that the only hope the Mid-Hants line had was to be similarly treated. But it was not to be so and other proposals, this time from the local councils, were put forward. The area was certainly in a growth situation, with new housing being developed at Springvale and at Alresford and Four Marks. Winchester Rural District Council offered £10,000 towards a halt being built for the Springvale residents, on the condition that the line remained open.

However, a renewed threat of closure brought with it another inquiry, this time at Winchester on 3rd July 1970. The TUCC heard many more objections, particularly on the capability of the bus operators being able to cope with the additional traffic. The TUCC's report to the Ministry of Transport stated that the area was expanding rapidly but did feel that the bus operators could cope with any extra passenger traffic. Parliamentary Under Secretary of State for Transport Industries at the Department of Environment, Eldon Griffiths, was quoted in local newspapers in early August 1971 as saying that the line was being assessed, "on a balance sheet of advantages and disadvantages". He continued, "by this I mean not only a saving for the taxpayer in terms of some £100,000 per year in grant aid (£135,000 costs less income of £31,000), but also in real resources of stock, staff and maintenance". Mr John Taylor, spokesman for the fighting group said, "that the quoted £100,000 was rubbish, as BR had themselves cut the expenditure amount to £88,000. The £31,000 income was calculated on an expected 7% increase in use of the line". John Taylor had evidence, following monthly checks on the line, that income was up 144% at Alresford alone during 1971. "We have proved over and over again that BR's figures for the line have been so removed from reality as to be fanciful", he claimed.

Mr F. Clifton Sherriff of Ropley and who subsequently went on to help preserve the line, said in the *Hampshire Chronicle* of 27th August 1971 that, "since the Public Inquiry days, the use of the line had risen by more than 140% and income was now in the region of £70,000 a year". He also suggested that, "the bus company would be unable to find the necessary extra services to carry an additional 1,000 passengers a day and that Hampshire County Council were going to be hard-pressed to find school buses for the youngsters who at present use the train".

It was a further year and a month before the Secretary of State for the Environment, Mr Peter Walker, announced his decision on 25th August 1971 based on the inquiry and it was to allow British Railways to close the line. Two further inquiries were forced by the objectors, aimed at the Traffic Commissioners and the bus company's application for licenses to operate the additional services. The first session of the inquiry, starting as it did on 26th October 1971, lasted four days and was resumed on 8th December 1971 for a further two days. Much of the time allocated at the hearing witnessed Mr Taylor cross examining Mr Dennis Flower of the Aldershot & District Traction Company on the ability of the Company to provide a bus service within the difficult times of adequate driving staff. It was also severely questioned whether the bus company could handle the anticipated large increase of passengers should the line close. In reality, it was stated, that not all passengers would take to the buses. It was of course evident that many would take to their motor vehicles. Time ran out again to continue the hearing and it was set to be re-convened for 2nd February 1972. The Mid-Hants line was reprieved for another Christmas.

At the end of the final ninth day of the inquiry, the chairman, Major-General A. F. J. Elmslie, said, "the inquiry has come to an end, but not to a conclusion". He told reporters that, "it would take some time to come to our decision, given the large amount of evidence and documents placed".

Meanwhile those who felt the line was not going to survive, started planning its future. During 1971 there were several suggestions as to a preserved steam line out of the failed Longmoor scheme, but this was not furthered. There were also suggestions as to a narrow gauge line and using the trackbed at Four Marks and Alresford for a by-pass. Within the whole closure framework, the County planners were also considering the planned M3 extension through the area and its consequences on the Winchester to Alton line, which it required to cross.

Then, on Monday 13th February 1972, the South-Eastern Traffic Commissioners announced their decision; that the bus services were going to be satisfactory. However, it was not to have any effect until any appeal arising out of the decision had been decided upon.

Needless to say, the objectors, which included the Rural councils at Winchester, Alton and Hampshire County Council, launched an appeal against the Commissioners judgement. The 1st and 2nd of August 1972 were set aside for the appeal hearing, which was held at the Rural Council's offices at Winchester. By now the objectors were trying to find anything to stop the line being closed and they fortunately found that the hearing in February had not taken into account the rail connections required by law for the bus services at Alton and Winchester.

Signalman Dennis Ford operates the mechanism to light up the gas light outside his signalbox at Alresford in November 1972. In two months' time he would shut off the light for good. *The late E.C. Griffith*

British Railways Board

WITHDRAWAL OF RAILWAY PASSENGER SERVICE

The Southern Region of British Railways hereby give notice that on and from Monday 5 February 1973 the railway passenger service between Alton and Winchester will be withdrawn and Medstead & Four Marks, Ropley, Alresford and Itchen Abbas stations closed. Details of the alternative bus services are available at local railway stations and bus offices.

The Winchester—Eastleigh/Southampton portions of the Alton trains will also be withdrawn on and from the same date. Details of the services remaining will be availabl[illegible] local stations shortly.

A poster put up at all the stations says it all.

But despite the appeal, the Secretary of State for the Environment, now Geoffrey Rippon of a conservative government, announced finally on 1st December 1972 that the railway could close after assurances of the bus alternative.

Fearing that this might well be the final decision, the objectors attempted to put together a subsidy scheme between the local councils. British Railways wanted £120,000 per annum to keep the line open and a minimum term of five years. By September 1972 the Roads and Bridges Committee of Hampshire County Council revealed that they could not recommend this subsidy payment to the Finance Committee. County officials reckoned that £52,000 would keep the

Above: The 'Hampshire Ferret' was a tour run on the last Saturday of operation, 3rd February 1973, and comprised two TC sets, Nos. 404 and 420, with No. 6511 as the power unit. The train went on to Southampton and Weymouth and is seen here coming into Alresford. *Below:* The last scheduled local service on the line was powered by 'Hampshire' DEMU No. 1130 leaving Alton at 2208 on 4th February 1973. *Both, Chris Small*

Above: The final passenger duty (a special run by BR at £1 per head) fell to Class 33 No. 6511 which departed from Alton after the last local service train had gone. Driver Charles Mitchell from Eastleigh was in charge, with Area Ticket Inspector Tony Thomas in the train. *Chris Small*

Left: A late-night photograph of the last local train as it prepares to depart from Alresford on 4th February 1973. The special (above) followed this service down the line. *The late E.C. Griffith*

railway running, but BR would not contemplate this line of argument.

Sir Richard Calthorpe, Chairman of Hampshire County Council, said that he would make representations to the Secretary of State for the line to remain "on strategic grounds". This proposal was put forward in November 1972 but came to nought.

One final attempt to halt closure proceedings was then exercised. The Ombudsman was asked by Miss Joan Quennell, MP for Petersfield, to investigate the whole situation because it was felt that inaccuracies had crept into the BR financial statements on the line's finances. One consultancy found out that some of BR's expenditure statements for the line were 40% more than they should have been and many of the income statements were thought to not include the whole receipts taken on the railway. Eventually the Ombudsman did release findings into the situation and criticised the government departments involved for not checking the figures from British Railways. Some of the BR statistics were reported to be wrong, but the report did not appear until August 1973, seven months after the line was closed.

Before the last train was scheduled to run, BR suggested that if they were guaranteed a minimum of £100,000 per year (the amount of subsidy given to BR by the DoE) from the local councils for a three year period, they would retain the link. Led by John Taylor, an effort was announced whereby the councils involved, Winchester Rural and City councils, Alton Rural District Council and Hampshire County Council, would put up £58,000. This was clearly short of the figure required by BR and the long battle to save the line was lost.

Five long years of objections and countless meetings had resulted in just a stay of execution. It was one of the most hard-fought and drawn-out battles to save a railway in Britain, likened perhaps more recently to the effort to save the Settle to Carlisle line in the late 1980s; happily this line survived intact.

The opportunity for local people, businesses and people travelling farther afield to make their journeys by railway and not being forced to use the road alternatives, was over and the last day of services was announced as 4th February 1973.

The Line Enters a New Era

Whilst the battle to save the line continued during 1972, it was announced in the railway press that a company, the Mid-Hants Railway Ltd, was negotiating with British Railways to save at least part of the line for a steam and local diesel service. It was thought the section from Alton to Alresford was the viable piece. Mr Simon Neave, from London, was at the head of this move and soon gathered interest amongst locals and enthusiasts alike. Soon after the line closed in the February of 1973, the new group was able to take over an office at Alresford station and the signalbox and begin their task of raising some £250,000 for the section to Alton.

Meanwhile, the County Council Finance Committee agreed to pay BR £13,650 a year for keeping the track in situ. Later in the February the Department of Environment announced that the M3 extension was to cross the line between Itchen Abbas and Winchester Junction and this was coupled with a new plan by the MHR Ltd, to try and secure the whole length of railway. John Taylor, who had fought for five years to retain the line in BR operation, also announced a group to try and secure the whole line, but initially only for a diesel service. The two groups then got together in May 1973 and formed the Winchester & Alton Railway Ltd and the Mid-Hants Railway Preservation Society Ltd to make a determined effort. History now takes us into the field of preservation and outside the parameters of the book. Suffice it to say that the line from Alresford through to Alton was secured and opened again for business as far as Ropley in April 1977.

One hundred and twelve years after the first opening day, the Mid-Hants Railway witnessed another jubilant celebration.

The line having been closed for over three years, diesel shunter No. 09003 hauls the last train over the old tracks of the Mid-Hants out of Alton on 6th March 1976. The vehicles would form the beginnings of the preservation scheme being set up between Alresford and Ropley.

R. W. Small

Just days after the last train, above, had passed over the line, the contractors moved in to remove the track. This is the scene in March 1976 near Mount Pleasant. The section of line west of Alresford towards Itchen Abbas was lifted shortly afterwards. *R.W. Small*

Bibliography

Bird John H., *Southern Steam Specials*, Kingfisher 1987.

Bradley D. L., *LSWR Locomotives* - three volumes Wild Swan 1986-7.

Casserley H. C., *London & South Western Locomotives*, Ian Allan 1971.

Cooper Peter, *LSWR Stock Book*, Kingfisher 1986.

Course E., *The Railways of Southern England: Secondary and Branch Lines*, Batsford 1974.

Dendy Marshall C. F., *History of Southern Railway*, Ian Allan 1982.

Griffith E. C., *The Basingstoke & Alton Light Railway*, Kingfisher 1982.

Holmes P., *Aldershot's Buses*, Waterfront 1992.

Lewis C., *Brief History of Mid-Hants Railway*, MHRPS 1977.

Mitchell V. and Smith K., *Branch Lines Around Alton*, Middleton Press 1984.

Pryer G., *Pictorial Record of Southern Signals*, OPC 1977.

Roberts E., *In and Around Alresford*, Laurence Oxley, 1992.

Stone R. A., *The Meon Valley Railway*, Kingfisher 1983.

Mid-Hants News, MHRPS, various issues 1976-1995.

Alton Herald; The Hampshire Chronicle, and *The Southern Evening Echo* - various issues.

The scene from the cab of 'Hampshire' DEMU No. 1127 as it approaches Alton station on 13th September 1972. The 'up' home signal is pulled off to allow the train to enter Platform 2. For the track on the right, it is the end of line for the old Meon Valley route. *Ron Neal*